Barking Mad in Barnstaple

Grace Dorey

Edited by Claire Makin

Illustrated by Claire Dorey

ryelands

To Nick, for giving me a bundle of fun.

To Claire, Martin, Jo, Maggie and Charlie
for being the best family in the world.

To all dog lovers who believe that puppy training is a walk
in the park and to those with experience who know it is not.

Originally published by Halsgrove
under the Ryelands imprint, 2008

Copyright Text © 2008 Grace Dorey
Illustrations © 2008 Claire Dorey

British Library Cataloguing-in-Publication Data
A CIP record for this title is available from the British Library

ISBN 978 1 906551 03 2

RYELANDS
Halsgrove House
Ryelands Industrial Estate
Bagley Road, Wellington, Somerset TA21 9PZ
Tel: 01823 653777   Fax: 01823 216796
email: sales@halsgrove.com
website: www.halsgrove.com

Printed in Great Britain by The Short Run Press, Exeter

CONTENTS

ACKNOWLEDGEMENTS

My gratitude goes to Glennis Hewitson for breeding my beautiful pedigree Golden Retriever puppy and for kindly letting me have him despite serious reservations.

I would like to thank my daughter, Claire Dorey, for her artistic illustrations of William crowning every chapter.

My thanks go to my son, Martin Dorey, my daughter-in-law, Jo and my grand-daughters, Maggie and Charlie for their support and for agreeing to star in the book.

I am indebted to my cousin, Claire Makin, for kindly using her professional talent to edit my book and produce the title and chapter headings.

A special thank you goes to my close friends Dorothy Gluck, Jenny Buchan, Ann Prior, Kay Crotty and Jennie Wonnacott for reading the script and for encouraging me to seek publication.

It was pure serendipity when Sue Blackmore from Towsers Country Kennels suggested that I should approach Halsgrove Publishing. So I am grateful to their Chairman, Steven Pugsley, for bravely publishing the diary which may, with a following wind, make William famous and go some way towards compensating for his year of wild behaviour verging on pure puppy pantomime.

Most importantly I would like to thank Nick for his total support in this venture, for sharing the amusing moments and for listening to the frequent tales of woe, but above all for believing that my therapy diary was not destined for the waste paper basket but would make an enjoyable read.

Grace Dorey

CHAPTER 1

WILLIAM ARRIVES

THE WEEK before I collected my adorable 'eat your heart out' Golden Retriever puppy, I learned with dismay that he had escaped from his cage and chewed through four computer cables as well as the mouse. Throwing caution to the wind and overcome with helpless emotion, I collected this delightful bundle of fluff on Valentine's Day and promptly named him William. He was ten weeks old. It was my first venture into becoming a proud puppy owner so I wisely signed up for all the puppy classes that Devon provided and devoured a range of expertly written dog training books. I also purchased a cage fit for a tiger and wondered if I had scrimped a little too much by not purchasing a lid.

Day One dawned like a miracle. It was a sunny Spring day and a joy to venture into my garden every hour with my new friend. He walked smartly to heel and refused to leave my side. We were best friends already. When he dumped a tiny deposit on the lawn I congratulated him as if he had performed a high-ranking circus act. There was nothing to this dog-training lark. After such a propitious start, all we had to do was continue in the same way. What a treasure. At night William was tucked into the corner of an enormous bed within his play pen and slept peacefully until 7.30am. What a star.

Day Two things started to deteriorate. The day dawned wet, cold and windy. William refused to pee up wind, down wind or indeed in any direction. I stayed outside until pneumonia beckoned and eventually returned to my cottage with a wet, soggy, smelly puppy who instantly pee-ed in the kitchen. I leaped for the bucket, mop and antiseptic, ignored the mistake and proceeded to clean my kitchen floor while

William pounced on the mop. Oh dear, things were starting to go downhill.

Feeding time for puppies occurs four times a day, a regime I found to be eminently suitable for humans too. William's extremely expensive puppy nuts contained every ingredient known to man and were guaranteed to produce a healthy hunky chap. These he refused point blank. I telephoned Glennis, my friend the dog breeder, who suggested a table-spoon of tuna with every meal. This worked a treat. The tuna was consumed and the puppy food remained defiantly in the shiny new dog bowl. Could a puppy develop into a fully grown dog solely on a diet of tuna? My puppy began to shrink and I started to panic.

Sunday lunchtime arrived and heralded my son, Martin, daughter-in-law, Joanne and two delightful granddaughters, Maggie and Charlotte aged four and two years. They pro-vided built-in entertainment for William. He became a bouncing lamb and on every bounce he leaked from his bladder and bowels. Clearly he had no control. Would he ever be able to spring without spurting or leap without plopping? He rolled on the lawn with the children, and this delightful cream-coloured furry animal became a mud-stained apology whilst whipping himself into circles of uncontrolled delight. He fol-lowed the grandchildren everywhere, I had lost my devoted companion, but was delighted that the family had bonded with the now most popular member of the family.

At lunchtime William smelt roast lamb, ignored his own food and waited patiently without begging at the table like a well-mannered dog. He was possibly too exhausted from his previous romp to move. I mixed some roast lamb with his own food and his appetite returned. Glennis dropped in to inspect William and found a grubby but happy puppy who had settled well into life in the fast lane. When my family left at 4pm William crashed out in his bed and slept peacefully without stirring until 7am the next morning.

The next day Barry, my gardener, arrived. He was requested to kindly mow the lawn as short as possible to prevent my toes getting wet through my sandals on the 7am shift. William showed no fear of the gardener or his lawnmower and pro-ceeded to assist with a little horticulture. He had to be restrained from gobbling the primroses, live-heading the daffodils and devouring fibre from the plant pots, but he successfully uprooted a newly planted fuschia, played havoc with the herb garden and dug holes with such ferocity that he could have bored for BP. Surely someone ought to be able to channel his enthusiasm into a usable energy source?

Over the next few days the blooms in the garden all disappeared; only the parsley was left standing and holes multiplied exponentially in the lawn and newly-dug beds, William became the unpaid gardener whilst I purchased some expensive canine shampoo.

Day Seven was a big day for William. He had an appointment with the vet for his second vaccination against every doggy ailment in the world. He threw up on the way to the vet and arrived looking like orphan Annie. He met his first cat in the waiting room and possibly imagined that these felines with those alluring eyes always came in boxes. He weighed in at 12.2Kg so was developing apace despite his fussy eating habits. He accepted his injection like a lamb, had both testicles felt and wowed the vet with his cuteness. My clever puppy was rewarded by being banned from leaving the confines of the garden for a week after this injection.

That evening he was invited to a puppy party at the local veterinary hospital. This visit was allowed. No doubt they were touting for business but also providing information about the hazards of round worms, tape worms, ticks and fleas; gruesome examples of which were duly passed round distastefully pickled in little jars. Fortunately these samples were long dead. It seemed that Devon was awash with these parasites and that the long grass particularly was alive with danger. Should William venture out at all?

En route to the socialization party William threw up from both ends in the car and arrived looking a veritable mess. Only one non-working sheepdog, Meg, looked grubbier. They became instant friends. For the rest of the evening William tried to hump Meg with all the expertise of a fully-grown hound. This did not bode well. If he displayed this behaviour as a young puppy what would he be like when he matured? To think that I had been concerned when I chose him that only one testicle had descended. At this rate he would be lucky to keep either of them.

When I collected William, Glennis told me that she had two similar puppies and that I could have the quiet docile one. I was sure that, like babies who get mixed up at birth, an error had occurred and that I had erroneously been slipped the mischievous brother. Certainly William was adventurous. He found gaps in the hedge bordering a field full of sheep and lambs unknown to my previous Retriever, Mischa. I was advised to carry the puppy up and down the steep steps to my cottage to spare his young hip joints. By Day Two William was bounding both up and down at high speed, completely fearless and without any consideration for his delicate hips. I immediately insured William as I could see a lifetime of trouble ahead.

Week Two started with a change of heart regarding William's insurance. I swiftly changed the policy from Norwich Union with a £50 excess to Marks and Spencer Pet Insurance which provided a cheaper plan with no excess. Hopefully even William would not use £7000 a year for his medical needs or in excess of £2 million for any damage he inflicted on a third party. So with a pet with more health insurance than myself (I had none), I anticipated the week ahead. There was one more week before we could venture to the park and explore the world outside. My garden was becoming rapidly bare and cavernous. William seemed to be digging his own grave. With my son's advice ringing in my ears: "I do not think you will be able to cope with a puppy. Why not have a fully trained adult dog?", I decided I needed help. So I started this diary as my therapy.

One of my friends, Sally, a Sex Counsellor (not mine) had written a diary from her puppy's point of view. However, I decided that it was I who needed the therapy, not William. He was a happy rascal who received unlimited stroking and cuddles whilst I was rewarded with a sense of failure in being unable to train his bladder and bowel. I travel the world teaching physiotherapists and nurses the intricacies of male and female pelvic floor dysfunction, but I was powerless to train a loveable fluffy puppy!

I had been desperately trying to accumulate newspapers to line William's cage and, more importantly, the boot of my car.

Previously discarded newspaper inserts now became a valuable commodity. The weekend papers were the best. I started to scrounge newspapers from my corner store. Apparently they always sent unsold papers back for a rebate but I was told I could take some of the freebies. So William commenced peeing on Agricultural Trader with impunity.

My kitchen became messy. It had a very clean floor smelling highly of Dettol to overpower the whiff of urine but it was littered with toys, yoghurt cartons and plastic packaging. William had the attention span of a mayfly and rapidly lost interest in each new gift. I kept a toy box for him similar to the one that I kept for the grandchildren where toys were rationed on a rotational basis, but he ignored most of these. His favourite pursuit was unravelling the raffia seat from under my chair in the kitchen - usually while I was eating. I was concerned that before long I would fall through or at least become extremely stuck. I was running out of objects to distract him sufficiently in order to enjoy a meal in peace and stay supported.

As it was a sunny day I decided William was going to have a photo-shoot. So armed with my mobile camera and a freshly brushed hound we descended into the garden. The cutie refused to pose. He refused to dig holes, trample the plants, smell the lavender or even lie doggo. Even David Bailey would have gone home.

Then William developed an egg on his head. It had grown slowly and I had tried to ignore it but now my puppy was metamorphosing into a unicorn. I imagined he had hit his head during one of his evening whirling dervishes under the kitchen table. These events always happened on a Sunday or Bank Holiday when the Vet was firmly closed. I brushed the dog, telephoned Glennis and invited her for tea. She assured me that this was a haematoma and that if it was aspirated it would refill with blood. I was unsure. Having seen many sports injuries in humans I knew haematomas could solidify and I did not want a bumpy puppy.

First thing Monday morning I took William to the vet. He bounded in eagerly: this was after all the puppy knocking shop. Fortunately there were no other puppies waiting to be humped so he behaved like an angel. That was until he saw the needle. The vet aspirated a little blood from his bump but reported that there was a bony knob underneath. Sadly William will be left with a bony bump which gives him rather a surprised expression where his fur stands on end, but hopefully this imperfection will become less noticeable as his skull grows. William was given some liquid antibiotic in a child proof (and granny proof) pot to mix with his dinner for a few nights. Fortunately he had finished having a cocktail of worm powder with his dinner so this would make a pleasant change. I deducted £30.98p for vet fees from his pocket money and wondered if Marks and Spencer would strike me off their insurance scheme if I submitted such an early claim.

My draining board now looked like a veritable veterinary clinic and smelt as pungent as a pet shop. It sported worm powder, antibiotic medicine, trial packs of puppy food, tins of tuna and a selection of tempting treats. It reminded me of the extensive needs of babies and their expensive requirements. This was the last day that William was confined to the garden.

He had improved in every department. He tucked into a corner of his enormous bed quite happily at 8pm (usually after going daft for an hour with fur and feathers flying in all directions) and slept through the night contentedly without barking. I cracked the early morning puddle in the kitchen by waking up at 6am and taking him straight out into the garden. He then pee-ed for England and received congratulations fit for a superstar before being lifted back into his pen whilst I hopped smartly back to bed. He was used to being in his play pen when I worked a three hour session at the hospital and did not seem distressed by my absence judging by the wonderful welcome I received when I returned. He had filled my life and was already giving me bundles of affection. He was my wonderful ball of fluff with a bump on the top.

William was learning fast. He had already learned what 'No' meant. 'No' meant do not eat the daffodils, 'No' meant do not attempt to chew the mower cable, 'No' meant do not jump up in the kitchen, 'No' meant do not unravel the raffia seat (any more) and 'No' meant I would rather you did not dig a hole there, but unsurprisingly this plea went unheeded. I used a range of distraction measures which mostly worked during the day but failed during his 'devil may care' evening hour when he charged menacingly from one sin to another with the speed of a recently released race hound.

William had grown. He was able to step out over the threshold of his play pen door without damaging his manhood but unsurprisingly preferred not to step back in. His legs had elongated up to his arm pits and failed to match his extra large bear-like furry paws. I imagined he was going to be big. I kept thinking of the adage 'Big feet, big .....' and worried about his rampant future ahead. Humpy Bumpy, the scourge of Barnstaple.

CHAPTER 2

TAMING THE BEAST

IT WAS A BIG DAY for William when we first ventured out down our Devon lane. He walked well on the lead to heel for a few hundred yards, making me a proud puppy owner. However, he soon discovered the sounds and smells of the countryside, paying particular attention to the ground level scents. The walk took ages as he had his own agenda. He smelt every living and rotting thing, he wanted to eat every twig and leaf and once he decided to roll in the middle of the road in joyous ecstasy. Amazingly, on the way back he had a homing instinct and galloped back up the hill to my cottage with his floppy ears flying in all directions. Since then he has displayed his love of the countryside by trying to escape through my five barred gate.

I went down to Homebase for yet more puppy food and noticed a roll of green plastic mesh which would be perfect for barricading my gate. Like most impetuous purchasers, I had not measured the gate but I estimated that it was three metres wide. I bought three and a half metres for good measure and meekly asked Michael, the guest in my 16th Century Barn if he would kindly tack it on for me. I provided the hammer and some staples and he immediately set to work. William assisted willingly by alternately scampering off with the hammer or the bag of staples. It was an incredible stroke of good fortune that the mesh fitted exactly. My gate became William-proof.

Sadly I had an engagement that had been booked prior to William's arrival to present male and female continence study days in Cork. So with a heavy heart I left William with Glennis's daughter, Carla; deposited his bed and a load of paraphernalia and departed for Ireland. On the way to Carla's house I drove at 20 mph to try to prevent Wills from throwing up. I looked in the mirror and found that I had collected a queue of about ten cars behind me travelling at this funereal pace.

This reminded me of two events. Firstly, when my dear father was in his late eighties he reported that he was always lucky on the Dorset roads because when there was a queue of cars he was always at the front. Secondly, it reminded me of my careful journeys to the foundry in Basingstoke with my wet clay sculptures ready to be cast in bronze. I was becoming my father. In retrospect I should have sported a notice in the back window saying 'Puppy aboard, might vomit'. In Ireland, my first presentation slide introduced a beguiling photo of William whom I used as an example of poor bladder and bowel control. William became an overnight sensation with the Irish Continence Physiotherapists. What a star. I missed him.

I also missed my first dog training class because my plane was five hours late leaving Cork due to a severe storm. A little plane that I feared was made of balsa wood with two dinky plastic propellers eventually arrived, and as we boarded we were sprayed, nay sloshed, with horizontal rain driven by gale force winds. I boarded this mechanical masterpiece full of fear and trepidation and thankful that I had recently written my will. The lady in the seat behind me hyperventilated for the whole flight but was completely ignored by the ashen airhostess who was not breathing at all. This meant that I had to stay alive in order to provide resuscitation to one or both of them as and when necessary. The pilot landed at Bristol on full throttle and managed to jam on the brakes just before we ran out of runway. I asked the pallid airhostess to congratulate the captain on a brilliant landing in such awful conditions and she said she would pass my message on when they were safely back in Cork! I imagine my comments never reached the pilot as she possibly collapsed or freaked out long before the flight back.

I arrived to collect William at 11pm, five hours late, with profuse apologies. I thanked Carla for kindly looking after my puppy and hoped to get a good report. He played well with Sky, Carla's female puppy, but Sky had failed miserably in teaching William to use the garden. I had so hoped that dogs would copy each other and perform in unison even though this trick had failed to work wonders in my garden when I had pee-ed beside my bladder- bound hound (of this more later!). William was presented to me highly shampooed, as were his blanket and his toys, due to a messy accident in his makeshift pen.

The next day I telephoned Tracey, the dog training guru, to apologize for not attending Session One of the dog training course. Undaunted, she insisted on 'getting me up to speed' by giving me a private lesson followed by hours of home-work. My burning question was how to deal with car sick-ness. These dog trainers are unreal. They work full-time, make no profit, receive no salary and lecture to schools and groups free of charge. Apparently my £50 course fee helped to pay towards printing the copious handouts and renting the premises at Chivenor Business Park. Tracey must have been on some type of wonder drug that kept her adrenaline charged. I have never known anyone so enthusiastic. Barbara Woodhouse paled by comparison. I thought physiotherapists were pretty energetic folk but dog trainers are in a class of their own, and believe that they can change the behaviour of the most wilful and disturbed hounds. This was just what William needed. He had met his match!

Whilst I was waiting for my private lesson, I watched Session Four of another class. William's sister, a diminutive, demure Retriever was receiving her guidance. She was sitting beautifully, learning to stay and learning to pass another dog without becoming excitable. She was extraordinarily well-behaved, looked cute and I wondered if I had been wise in choosing a dog puppy.

On arriving home I read the car sickness leaflet. Dear me! I should open all the doors of my car and for the first week I should let Wills play inside. Not in my new car! I had spe-cially bought a Volkswagen Golf hatchback and dog guard so that Mischa, my previous Golden Retriever could ride in the back in style. So this same area was firmly allocated to William. The second week we should play in the car together but I should gradually close the doors one at a time. The third week I should start the car and drive up and down the drive. If the car sickness returned we should start the regime all over again. Poor Wills would be prevented from attending the second puppy party, prevented from visiting the vet and unable to visit the Millennium Green in Landkey. Not that he had yet ventured as far as the Green due to his acute dislike of leads. He would scratch his neck in an attempt to remove the collar, looking as if he was killing fleas. When I walked him down my lane he would stop, roll over and refuse to budge, often in the middle of the road. We would never get far in any park at this rate.

Off we went again to the vet's to see Katya. I lifted him onto the table and watched the two of them bonding well. William received his anti-rabies vaccination and microchip like a lamb in preparation for receiving his passport in six months time, provided that the blood test in three weeks time proved satisfactory and his antibodies increased to 0.51U/ml. The bill was an astounding £171, which was sadly not covered by his £199 annual medical insurance. My salary seemed to be going puppywards at an alarming rate. I must be barking; all this for a puppy who may not have conquered his travel sickness when he receives his passport. In fact he could leave the country now but would be refused re-entry.

Once outside the surgery William was unable to maintain his previous level of dignity. He sat down on the pavement then superglued himself to the road in the car park and stalwartly refused to move. Part of this behaviour was due to his wearing a collar and being attached to a lead, but part of it was a stubborn 'see if you can move me from here' streak. Whilst he was stationary, a delightful little girl of four years of age asked if she could stroke the puppy. William turned on the charm, adored the attention and positively glowed. He was in his element and the superglue dissolved.

In the afternoon my recently chipped puppy was introduced to the two Labradors, Jessie and Penny, owned by my neighbours, John and Louise. These two adult female dogs were three times the size of William. He was in heaven, sniffing, chasing, circling and even rolling on to his back in a fully submissive pose with his 'lipstick' fully erect. I was particularly pleased with this new friendship as my previous

Retriever, Mischa, had always been frightened of these dogs and had barked at them furiously at every opportunity.

The reason I wanted a puppy and not a fully grown dog was primarily so that I could train the puppy myself and eliminate dear Mischa's faults. These were numerous. She pulled on the lead so that my arm nearly came out of its socket. It was all I could do to hold the lead when she was setting out determinedly for a walk. Many was the time that she pulled me downhill at a pace not befitting a granny. Infuriatingly, when my cousin's daughter Julia was 10 years old she walked Mischa down the same route without pulling and with a slack lead! When I walked up a hill and needed a little assistance she rather annoyingly stopped pulling. Regularly Mischa would bark furiously at the Labradors living opposite, bark when I was on the telephone and bark herself hoarse and jump vertically to greet new arrivals. Some of her barking was protective. She would bark if anyone tiptoed past my house. I needed no burglar alarm, no door knocker or bell and I always knew when letters and parcels arrived. However, it was reported to me that she stayed silent and off duty when I was out and the window cleaner or gardener appeared.

My four year old grand-daughter Maggie could not pronounce William and called him 'Willywam' which was the same name as her boyfriend at school. Judging by the way William (the puppy not the boyfriend) behaved, Maggie may have been more perceptive than we thought! Maggie and her sister Charlie, my darling granddaughters, came to look after William whilst I received an appraisal for my post as Professor of Physiotherapy (Urology) at the University of the West of England, Bristol. I filled out the necessary forms pertaining to teaching continence to humans but refused to divulge my failure to train my loveable, fluffy hound. Having said that, William had cottoned on to the idea of holding out until morning for a pee, although he sometimes stirred at 5.30am and pee-ed a small lake. His bowels were performing nicely in the garden after breakfast. Yes, he was still having some accidents but he was still a puppy with normal puppy foibles.

The time came for us to attend the second puppy party at the Vet's. I was relieved that Wills suffered no car sickness, just a little light diarrheoa, so he smelt high as a kite when we arrived. There were two Golden Retriever puppies present, a brother and sister, who were two weeks younger and considerably smaller than Wills, which made me realize how much he had grown. His diet of tuna, pedigree puppy food, gravy bone biscuits and roast chicken treats were building a fine hound. At this rate his skull would soon grow around his bump!

William was delighted to see Meg the Collie again, especially as she had made such an effort to arrive shampooed, sweet smelling with teeth gleaming. However, he was far from pleased when Jack the Jack Russell, a quarter of her size, took over William's humping role and then lay in a submissive pose whilst Meg licked his lipstick. What a fickle bitch.

This class was designed more for puppy owners than for their pets. If puppies ate their poo, we were told not to clear up in front of them in case they felt possessive and wanted to gobble it up faster. We were warned that newspaper in the kitchen gave puppies permission to pee, which was something that I had already learnt from bitter experience. We were emphatically told never to say 'No' but to distract the puppy from biting the furniture and running off with slippers, gloves and tea-towels. It was our fault if we wore a floating dressing gown as this was an invitation for the puppy to sink his teeth into it and hold on. This explained why Tracey was dressed in black leggings and a black sweat shirt reminiscent of Max Wall. What was one supposed to wear for the 5.30am shift? If the darlings jumped up, we were to turn our back on them, presumably so they could jump up our backs. I was extraordinarily relieved to hear that it was normal for puppies to go berserk and generally run amok at 6.30pm, the time when William zig-zagged across the garden visiting every boundary by crashing straight through the flower beds and adding depth to his network of holes. Apparently digging is normal for wild dogs who live in tunnels often as long as eight feet. William would soon be able to dwell outside at the rate he was digging.

All the puppies in the class were young and between eight and 12 weeks of age. They were an eclectic group with some breeds so small that they arrived in a pocket. We were told that the puppy stage was transient, whereupon we all sighed, but, and this was a big but, this was nothing compared with the teenage years which lasted from 20 weeks to two years. Still, I reckoned by that time William would be living in self-fashioned underground accommodation.

Those of us who were blessed with children or grand-children were warned not to let the children rush around and chase the puppy, not to roll around together, never to lie down and be submissive to a dog and certainly not to play chasing or tugging games. The training had to be consistent. Dogs were not allowed to jump up. They were to be walked sedately by child or adult. We were shown a shocking photograph of the badly scarred face of a dear little boy and were warned that if a dog growled and the child continued to advance, it would be the child's fault not the dog's if their face was scratched.

With this warning ringing in my ears, William and I ventured out to the Millennium Green. Progress was fearfully slow: he smelled every blade of grass, ate every twig and progressed at his own sluggish pace. At times he sat down refusing to budge and at other times he rolled over out of pure 'joie de vivre'. Everything changed when he met other dogs and the party commenced. He became a sociable animal, madly inquisitive and helplessly appreciative of all four-legged friends and their owners. As 'the new kid on the block' he welcomed the adoring attention as if he was starved of affection at home.

Then to my horror William made a bee-line for a tiny tot toddling across the other side of the green. I panicked, imagining visions of my overgrown and exuberant puppy flattening the innocent infant – or worse. I yelled "Pick up your baby!" to the surprised father in authoritative tones reminiscent of Hyacinth Bouquet from 'Keeping Up Appearances' as my hound bounded up like a lion for the kill. Fortunately the young father swept his daughter up out of harm's way just in time to avert bloodshed. (Happily, both the drive to the Green and the return journey were vomit-free although I would have liked William to have paid more attention to rear end control.)

Today I completed my homework. I read two booklets and

one handout all of which emphasised puppy training by learned good behaviour using a clicker and a reward system. For example, at the command of 'Sit' William should sit and I should 'Click' and then reward him with a nibblet. William took to this like a duck to water. Previously he had been commanded to 'Sit' and sit he did. Now he was faring even better with a click of recognition and a treat. Having grasped Lesson One I decided to advance to Lesson Two with 'Lie, Click, Reward'. William was more creative here and added 'Lie, Click, Roll, Paws bent in begging position looking cute' for his unforthcoming reward.

Bad behaviour was to be ignored by turning our back on the misdemeanor. Pretty difficult when William was hell bent on unraveling the raffia seat, re-arranging the garden, eating a bumble bee or attempting to escape through the five-bar gate. In these scenarios we were advised to offer another more exciting toy. Easier said than done. What is more exciting than destroying the furniture? Guess chicken would suffice, but would that look as if he was receiving a treat for biting the kitchen to bits? Choke chains were not permitted, corporal punishment was forbidden and no shouting was allowed. In my naiveté I had been guilty of yelling "Down" like a fishwife when William had tried to leap upstairs or launched himself at a hot roast chicken on the working surface. William was going to attain doghood with regular training, kindness and rewards. If one treat failed to reward sufficiently we could reward exceptionally good behaviour with a jackpot bonus of treats. I couldn't help thinking that the clicker company and the treat industry were both in league here, making a handsome profit from all the clever and cunning puppies in the world.

CHAPTER 3

NOT SO CUTE

ON MARCH 5th 2007 William was three months old. He was a joy and delight and enhanced my life. I looked at him sometimes and saw the same dreamy brown eyes that Mischa used to melt my heart, except that William's eyes were framed below with a pure white crescent which gave him an even more appealing and adorable look. Mischa was no relation, so mercifully Wills would not inherit her barking and tugging genes. As my friend Glennis was a breeder of Golden Retrievers, I was able to order a designer puppy. I chose Reggie to be the sire and Emma to be the dam. Reggie was selected because he was a gorgeous champagne-coloured dog who was well-mannered, quiet and small. Emma was chosen as she was a proven mother with a demure, docile disposition. Neither barked, neither tugged, so I hoped for the perfect dog. Being realistic, I craved for the same company and deep devotion that I received from Mischa for eight years during my time in Devon.

After a swift courtship which did not include dinner, Reggie and Emma rekindled their relationship with feeling. They mated once, twice and then thrice just for the hell of it. William was the product of a loving if not prolonged relationship. Nine weeks later six little puppies arrived. I could not keep away. I visited the puppies every week from the time that their eyes were tight shut to the time when they were ready for homing. They were gorgeous. My grandchildren, Maggie and Charlie, were regular visitors and similarly smitten. The puppies doubled in size every time I set eyes on them. They were all so cute and playful. It was difficult to choose between them.

The soft fur on a puppy is one of the most exquisite tactile sensations. No wonder dogs are used as therapy for the elderly and the infirm. When I was a small child on holiday in Eastbourne (we knew no other resort) I used to be reprimanded by my mother for stroking elderly ladies' fur coats and severely warned not to stroke their Pekinese dogs in case they amputated my fingers. However, I always thought the risk was worth it. When I chose cats I selected the furriest breed possible. Before I moved to Devon, when I was working full-time as a Physiotherapy Manager at BUPA Hospital Bushey, I had two Persian cats bred from champions: a male who sported a glorious thick white coat and a female who was fluffy blue. I loved them. Oscar, the large white male, was quite a character and never passed the refrigerator without attempting to open it just in case someone had left it unlocked. Yes, we had to design a 'fridge lock after a leg of lamb was mysteriously stolen in the night. Ruffles, the blue Persian, arrived first and never ever came to terms with Oscar's presence. She would bat him across the head when he came in through the cat flap after spending a night on the tiles (maybe a tad jealous?). When he was taken to the Vet she would move pointedly into his basket in the vain hope that he would not return. This fur fetish never left me. I must admit I am still unable to pass any furry material in a department store without deviating to stroke it.

My new furry friend excelled himself on the 11th March 2007 by pee-ing to order outside on each occasion and sustaining no accidents indoors. The day started at 5.30am and he was taken out after each meal, drink and quiet time. This was a cause for celebration though I was realistic enough to suspect that this behaviour would not continue if there was a howling gale. I delayed any flag flying until he had poo-ed regularly outside too.

Then I transported a reluctant puppy to Canine Etiquette, his new school. We were the last to arrive (due to an emergency clean-up operation at the gate prior to entering). Wills was the largest lad in the pack and the only one with a single parent owner. All his other classmates were accompanied by complete families with 2.4 children. For them this was a delightful family outing, and for children a preferable activity to Brownies and Cubs. I was the oldest owner by about 30 years and by the end of the evening everyone knew William by name. I was given a purple clicker and a bag of similarly coloured liver cubes and asked to practise 'Command, Click, Reward'. William became hyper on liver and displayed the wilful side of his character in front of all the other obedient puppies. He had a variety of tricks. He allowed the two Boxer brothers to slobber all over him, he kissed the little Spaniel front and back and then sat on him, he out-barked Tracey during the lecture. Then by way of encore he lay on the floor prone with legs akimbo and edged himself forwards on his belly using his elbows to reach the toys in the middle of the room as if no-one could see him. A boy of about 11 years old who was accompanying the flattened spaniel, and attending under extreme sufferance, whispered loudly to his mother: "William is a proper dog, couldn't we have a dog like him?".

I arrived back from William's school with eyes pricking. It may have been the drying effect from the heat in the room but it felt mightily like conjunctivitis. I lay in bed at night opening and closing my eyes and pondering the blinking problem. It would be catastrophic if I became allergic to fur.

The next day I was taking my pants and tights downstairs to the washing machine when my monster puppy tugged them away from me and raced around the kitchen with my precious tights flying like streamers. From my training I had two choices; either I could find a more exciting toy (impossible) or I could turn my back on him and show complete indifference to him and my underwear. I knew that I should not chase him around and make this debacle into a game, and I was not allowed to shout. I reluctantly turned my back on my holey tights and a gleeful William who showed blatant disregard for my personal not-so-smalls. Game, set and match to Wills, but my fault for allowing this to happen.

Far worse was to follow. It gives me great pain to report that my lovely puppy has just badly bitten me. As I type this I can feel my finger throbbing rhythmically. Last night I found William eating some lamb bones which Michael, my Barn guest, had thrown into the flower bed for the foxes (with no regard to the well-being of the free-range chickens across the road!). I removed two bones from William's mouth then he seemed to get a rib bone stuck to the roof of his mouth. I tried to remove the bone and William's needle-like teeth bit right through the middle finger on my right hand, straight through the nail until the tip of my finger was hanging by a small piece of skin. I suffered from indignant shock and dialled my son, Martin, who dialled 999 and within 15 minutes an ambulance arrived.

The paramedics Colin and Rob were excellent, very kind and extremely understanding, and wanted to know if they had to search for a finger tip. My blood pressure shot up to an all time high. They saw William sitting in his cage looking demure and (I hope) contrite, and thought that butter would not melt in his mouth. I was not so sure. I was taken to the North Devon District NHST Hospital, which is one of the places where I work, and waited and waited. There were twenty people in distress. I sat next to a man who had almost lost a finger to a circular saw, and on the other side to a farmer who had injected his finger accidentally with black spot vaccine when one of the cows moved whilst he was immunizing 60 of them using the same needle. We became the 'finger row' all sitting there with our fingers raised rather rudely. Martin arrived most thoughtfully with a magazine, and we waited and waited with no ability to concentrate on the television or cope with reading.

The NHS statistics only count waiting time to see the triage nurse which was under an hour, and not the total wait. She berated me for calling an ambulance, which might have been required for a more needy case, instead of arriving by taxi. I reminded her that my son called the ambulance and that I had not called one for 50 years since I broke my leg on the back of a motor bike on the first date with my ex-husband, also that I considered I was not a drain on the Health Service, particularly as I worked there too. I thought she must have skipped charm school and missed out on the patient care lectures. The two doctors were rushed off their feet and through the flapping curtains it was possible to hear every conversation, every complaint and everyone complaining.

The casualty medical officer thought I should have my finger dressed with steri-strips, have a tetanus injection and receive a massive supply of antibiotics. I was written up for a triple injection for tetanus, polio and typhoid even though I was up to date with my anti-tetanus prophylaxis. When I asked the nurse about the side-effects of this injection, she replied "I haven't a clue". Four hours later my son drove me home telling me again that he thought I was irresponsible to have a puppy. I gathered he thought I was barking mad too. Not a good day!

There were two reasons why Martin was so against me having a puppy. Firstly he felt it would be too much for me and secondly he felt that I was away from home too much. The first reason I am sure was based on his experience with the puppy that he chose and I bought for his birthday; a tiny little black and white Jack Russell named Paddy, who travelled back from the breeder in a hat (not wearing it, in it!). That was the only time that Paddy was demure. He grew up to be a champion biter. He would nip ankles, latch on to trousers and worst of all latch on to Mischa's neck for a ride every time she left my kitchen. Mischa was too gentile to snarl at him and play top dog. Paddy was King, feared and fearless.

When I looked after him I had to get out of bed in the morning straight into my Wellington boots to prevent my ankles from being shredded to ribbons. I kept booted up for all the chores, especially whilst I was washing up. Mischa used to dread these visits when her tranquil life would be re-arranged by a dog a fifth of her size. One time when Martin and Jo were away and I was preparing to lecture abroad, I was asked to take Paddy to the kennels where they also had a Jack Russell named Treacle who enjoyed total freedom circling the farm perimeter. Paddy stuck to his new-found friend for a week; together they ignored the other dogs on the twice daily walks and happily chased around the extensive farm together. They were inseparable. I asked the kennel owners if they would like to keep Paddy as a friend for Treacle. Unhappily, the story did not end there. When Martin and Jo returned from holiday they received a telephone call out of the blue from the kennel owners saying that they had found a new home for Paddy. It took less than five minutes to find the culprit and I still blame the kennel owners for disclosing my identity. I was not popular for even suggesting that Paddy should be re-homed.

Sadly the time came when Martin and Jo did need to find a new home for Paddy. Their daughter Maggie, aged just one year, was diagnosed with acute myeloid leukaemia and admitted to Bristol Children's Hospital for six months. My darling granddaughter experienced the ravages of chemotherapy while we took turns to be with her during the day and sleep with her at night in the hospital. She was never left alone. Fortunately Maggie responded well to treatment and has developed into a gorgeous four-year-old girl with long blonde hair which she refuses to have cut. At that time it was a kind and brave decision when Martin and Jo gave Paddy to a farmer friend named Freddie. They decided that a Jack Russell should not be confined to a garden but have freedom and open spaces in which to pursue the sport of ratting. Soon Paddy accompanied Freddie everywhere. They travelled miles together, either by foot, four by four or tractor. Freddie adored Paddy who has certainly earned his keep many times over as the world's best rat catcher.

When I returned from the hospital I telephoned my special friend Nick (the love of my life who had kindly and generously given me my puppy) and plaintively announced "My Christmas present has just bitten me!". Nick was most upset and concerned about my finger. I reassured him that I had been vaccinated against tetanus (again) and was sensibly taking my antibiotics. I assured him that this dog was not just for Christmas but for life. I did say that I would not be removing bones wedged in William's mouth again but would visit the Vet the next time. Apart from this one incident William had not been a biter. In fact when Tracey of Click Club fame gave him a treat she commented on his particularly soft mouth.

The day after the injury, I came to terms with not driving and, even worse, not playing tennis, and gradually became more adept at dressing, preparing food, washing up and typing with my throbbing finger held high. How could anyone think I could be without William? It was not his fault. The fault was mine. I would protect him to the ends of the earth, but this did not prevent me from spending the day well away from his sharp end.

The next day William relinquished his crocodile image to resemble that of a Dalmation. He had either played with a sack of coal or he had developed Black Spot. I declined to bathe him in order to spare my bandage from a soaking. Later, I popped down to the GP Practice Sister to have my dressing changed. The finger looked a mess – and so did William - but at least I had a new clean white bandage.

On Mother's Day, Martin and Jo invited me for lunch and a walk with William. Jo is the world's best mother to my darling granddaughters. I arrived with an apple crumble proudly made with one hand - a triumph and quite unlike my numerous culinary disasters which resembled the efforts of Wendy Craig in 'Butterflies'. I can remember once when I overcooked three pizzas and announced to the family: "Don't worry I'll have the burnt one". To which Martin replied: "Mum, they're all black!".

We were destined to visit Westward Ho!, the only town in the UK sporting an exclamation mark. It would have been William's first sighting of the sea. As there were gale force winds, the organised day of beach cleaning by the residents was cancelled so we decided to go for a more sheltered walk. Wills was a super puppy all day. At their home he played with Maggie and Charlie and they learned some valuable lessons. They were taught to leave puppies alone during feeding, not to lie down and get lower than a dog (that indicates submission), and to leave William alone when he was settled and resting (let sleeping dogs lie!). William was confined to the conservatory during lunch but allowed out into the garden to pee. I was proud of my mutt who repaid me by peeing outside to the command of 'Be a good boy', and keeping the house dry.

Unfortunately his tail end was not so controlled in Martin's car on the way to a beautiful walk along the river Torridge, starting from Northam. We met four people resting on a seat who were obviously starved of puppy love. William stood in front of each one in turn allowing them to stroke him whilst lapping up all the attention. When we arrived at a beach area we let him off the lead and he immediately made friends and dominated a petite Jack Russell named Holly who could outrun a greyhound and jump higher than a grasshopper. Eventually Holly leapt a metre high on to a wall to be with her owners for safety, leaving William totally perplexed and a tad envious.

This outing was an eye-opener. William could actually walk. Not only that but he could walk to heel without pulling or stopping. He enjoyed the company of the children as much as they enjoyed being with him, and when they took his lead, the lead went slack so it dangled in the mud. This was what having a dog was all about. It enhanced our walk and made a very special and memorable family day in a beautiful part of North Devon.

That night there were gale force winds and driving hail more akin to a blizzard in the Antarctic than to Spring weather in the West Country. At 7am William stirred, much later than usual, presumably due to exhaustion from his walk the previous day, and indicated that he would like to go outside. This was a first. He had never asked before. I muffled up in my Barbour, cosy mohair hat, fur lined glove on my left hand and woollen sock on my right hand, and ventured into the garden with William. I stood in the entrance to the wood-shed with Wills whilst he reviewed the situation. Then he was off. Not to pee but to devour the hailstones. I deserted him and rushed inside out of the icy wind. When eventually he scratched on the door to be admitted he was covered in hail-stones and resembled a happy husky ready at a moment's notice to go to the South Pole.

The next day the fierce winds continued, making puppy training a sport for mad dogs and Englishmen. William would dump and run back into the house, or pee and hurtle back. Even he failed to find any enthusiasm for walking in a gale.

Then we prepared for the Clicker Club. William had failed to practise his clicking homework (possibly because I had not clicked sufficiently) but he sat to order, lay down to order and stood to order when he was ready. Tracey took the register and with a booming voice called "William" to which he responded with an equally loud "Woof" to the amusement of the assembled class. I could see now I was going to own a clown, the one who would disrupt the most orderly of students. And disrupt he did. Holly, his new Jack Russell friend from Northam beach, arrived and sat next to him. Wills continued the domination theme from their previous encounter, kissed fore and aft and then lay on top of her so that this cute little dog completely disappeared from sight leaving only her black tail with the white tip on view wagging furiously. Tracey asked the owners if anyone had problems with biting. I was the only honest one there and held my bandaged finger aloft. This was wisely ignored but it did cause a titter round the room.

We learned walking to heel one at a time with Sally in a partitioned part of the room behind a curtain. William excelled at this task and I was both amazed and proud in equal measure. Rather like my own offspring he could raise his game during examinations. What a clever bunny.

A week after William bit the hand that fed him I thankfully finished taking the gaudy yellow and red Amoxicillin and humongous white lozenge shaped Augmentin. The difficulty with pills was not only remembering them but also worrying about any possible side-effects. Waking up with a claggier mouth than usual was dealt with speedily by vigorous teeth cleaning after the all too familiar early morning visit outside. William's teeth were another problem. I was given some free toothpaste for dogs but felt it a little unwise to be attending to his deadly fangs, at least until my finger had healed. William will have to learn not to bare his grubby teeth in company.

Wills was more than happy to bare his teeth and smile at the free range farm chickens clucking and strutting across the road so I asked Barry my gardener if he could kindly erect a wire fence to prevent him (William not Barry) from falling down a twenty foot drop from my garden onto the road. In one burst of enthusiasm either William would be injured or the chickens would be lucky to survive. I had learned the hard way that dogs and chickens do not mix. I was looking after a beautiful well-trained Golden Retriever two years ago, and whilst we were walking up the lane past the farm she made a dive for a chicken walking across the road, which immediately keeled over. The farmer was even less pleased than the chicken even though this perceived ignominy was a clear example of a road kill. I sent the farmer a note of profuse apology enclosing £5 (more than the going rate for a chicken) and received no reply. I subsequently heard that the plucky hen had lived so it was comforting to know that I was £5 in chicken credit.

It seemed as if two chickens showed complete indifference to the shiny new fence. The same day that it was erected the mad hens flew in and started to goad poor William who bounced after them as fast as his growing legs could carry him, leaving a trail of fur, feathers and foliage across the lawn. One flew away but the less expert of the pair chickened out and scuttled around the garden with William's nose up her tail feathers until she eventually squeezed through some blackberry brambles (the home to a thousand rabbits) to safety. Since then William has made a more concerted effort to hunt hens and I feared this may be a prelude to a less fortunate episode.

I have noticed that along with the bump on his head William has another imperfection. Perhaps these identity marks ought to feature on his passport along with his chip and pin. His tail seems to be kinked in the middle. I have examined it from a distance and from a number of oblique angles and it may have been just a rogue curl of fur but I had watched his tail develop on a daily basis. It wagged very well, meaning that he had the use of his right and left ischio-coccygeus muscles and he was exercising these muscles regularly, but he still did not have the strength to lift his tail aloft, rather it arched downwards akin to a limp handshake, and there was this kink in the middle. I had not shut his tail in the door nor do I believe had anyone else. Wills was the only one who had played havoc with his tail and shown it no mercy. He could bite it and spin clockwise or anticlockwise as the mood took him, gaining in speed and pivoting around an imaginary central spot, a performance which would impress even the harshest of ice-dance judges. He could even spin round, tail in mouth, in his play-pen without touching the sides. Also his tail seemed to be too long for a puppy which was rather worrisome. So my questions were: "Will he grow to fit his tail and will he be able to get it up?".

Recent research by Professor Vallortigara and colleagues at Italy's Bari University reported in the journal 'Current Biology' in 2007 that dogs wag their tails to the right when they see something familiar and to the left when they are frightened and about to retreat. I was sceptical and decided to investigate using William as a sample. My clever pet was a right wagger; his tail did not even cross the mid-line indicating that he was delighted to see me. Apparently the research in Italy showed that a sunny disposition is associated with greater activity in the left hemisphere of the brain which controls the right side of the body. So a happy and contented hound will have a more developed right ischiococcygeus muscle.

A HEART-RENDING
DECISION

YESTERDAY MARTIN, Maggie and Charlie arrived unannounced. It was lovely to see them. William was uncontrollably boisterous. He jumped up at both the little children despite pleas to sit. Gradually he calmed down and the children threw toys for him to fetch, with some success. Suddenly he bit the sleeve of little Charlie's cardigan and refused to let go. I had to prise the sleeve out of William's mouth. This scary incident was enough to put Charlie, who was only two years old, off dogs for life. I am now terrified that the next time it could be her small arm or face, and that she could be scarred for life. I spent a sleepless night agonising over what I should do for the best. I would never ever forgive myself if one of my darling granddaughters was harmed and I must say that I have been very twitchy and overcautious ever since William bit me.

I rang Glennis and related what had happened. She said that she had worried about me every day because having grandchildren calling occasionally makes a puppy extremely excitable, and that this is a different scenario from having children in the house all the time. She reminded me that she was not happy with me having a puppy in my situation. She suggested that I had two options: either to re-home the puppy (which would be very easy but choked me up) or to keep William in his play pen whilst the children were around for six months until he was older. These were decisions I was desperate not to confront. I become extremely emotional at the thought of losing my best friend. He was a healthy and normal puppy with a tuft on his head, a kinky tail and just a tad of dandruff. I was unable to make any decisions that day.

I went to the GP practice nurse to have my dressing changed yet again and to my horror, three days after finishing the course of antibiotics, I saw the finger was grossly infected. The lovely sister called a doctor who prescribed me even larger Augmentin bombs, this time for ten days, but left with a salutary warning. If I had red streaks travelling up my arm, if I felt faint, vomited or had a headache I was to visit Accident and Emergency immediately. This was not good as I had just posted a letter to the Director of Nursing complaining about the lengthy wait and the lack of patient care received in A&E, which after all was the window to the hospital where I worked.

I telephoned my daughter Claire and in tears related William's incident with little Charlie. Claire said she would support me in whichever decision I made. Claire had been particularly close to Mischa who had followed her about like a large fluffy lapdog. Once, when we walked down to The Castle Inn in Landkey, I left Claire with some friends in the pub and took Mischa back home with me to prepare roast lamb for lunch. Mischa walked two paces, stopped and looked round waiting for Claire to join us. Progress home was slow as Mischa repeated this behaviour all the way back over a three mile distance.

I telephoned my son Martin and discussed the two available options that Glennis had somberly suggested. Martin wanted me to know that he and Jo would support me either way. I was warmed and heartened to receive the support of both my children, but I was still unsure what I should do for the best.

Full of emotion I then telephoned Nick who decided to come down to Devon to visit that week. This meant that I could postpone any major decisions until his visit, when I hoped I would be able to think more clearly.

I visited the Vet to purchase some more worming powders in case dandruff was in any way related to systemic worms. The receptionist noticed my finger and we digressed by discussing dog bites in detail. She had been bitten by one of her dogs five months ago when she had tried to separate them in a fight, and she proudly showed me her distorted nail which had only just completely regrown. It seemed as if Barnstaple was a haven for biting dogs. Earlier when I had spoken to the GP he said that I was his fifth dog bite victim that morning. Perhaps we should form a victim support group.

Meanwhile Glennis arrived to help bathe the dandruffed William as I was unable to undertake this exercise with my wounded finger. We discussed puppy behaviour and the difference between living with little children (where the puppy becomes used to having little ones in the home all the time) and the scenario when the puppy gets boisterous and overexcited when little ones come to visit at intervals. Glennis felt that if I confined William to his play-pen when Maggie and Charlie came round, he would gradually grow out of this puppy behaviour. Also she felt that the dog training classes we were attending would definitely help.

She arrived on cue to meet William who had been splashing, nay wallowing, in a large muddy drinking trough by the side of the barn and had emerged a decidedly darker shade of pale. One grubby puppy! Perhaps this was the treatment for dandruff in the wild. This was his lucky day: two treatments for the price of one, orthodox and unorthodox, but it was anybody's guess which one was which. Obviously research was urgently needed. Perhaps Professor Vallortigara and his pals could pick up the gauntlet. They could give William a central parting and apply a mud pack on the right side and puppy shampoo on the left and then assess the fur for reduction of dandruff, silkiness and bounce.

Glennis asked me for the garden hose. Alas, William had made sure that this could not be used for soaking him. My playful hound had previously wrenched the hosepipe from the tap, chewed the connection and punctured it profusely, rendering it unfit for purpose. William was caught red-handed a week before so was not able to pass the blame on to anyone else. Glennis and I started operations by covering the drinking trough with the folded pasting table and placing a rock on the top for good measure. Subsequently I ordered a slab of slate to cover the trough and fashion a garden seat. Then with buckets of warm water we bathed the mucky pup, lathered him generously with the best 'shampoo for puppies and kittens', rinsed him thoroughly in every nook and cranny, cuddled him dry in a large towel and dared him to get muddy again - ever. It was at this point that I knew that William and I could not, would not, be parted. He had entered my life, indeed become a major part of my life; he was my best friend and I unashamedly loved him.

Nick telephoned to see if I was less weepy. I told him about my big decision to keep William and he intuitively and kindly commented that he thought I had not been thinking straight the day before. He also said that if I had decided to re-home William he would have taken him to his home in Ireland for a while until he had calmed down and grown more responsible. This thoughtful and generous offer warmed my heart. It seemed as if everyone I had spoken to wanted to help me to keep my new pal. I felt so much happier and reassured that I had made the right decision.

Nick called me the next night to discuss dog training packages. He had admired the intelligent and obedient dogs produced from gun dog training and was prepared to investigate the possibilities in Devon. I on the other hand have a loathing of guns. I am a pacifist and was averse to letting my dog join a shooting party. I also disliked the idea of packing William off to boarding school even though I may have been allowed weekend visits. I said that I would enquire about intensive training packages from Canine Etiquette on Monday.

The clocks have gone forward! I have been looking forward to this day for two weeks as William's 5.30am early morning call will now be a civilised 6.30am, provided that he fails to twig the intricacies of British Summer Time. Today I visited a packed Garden Centre to purchase a new garden hose encased in a dog proof cover, three Lavateria plants to hide the newly erected fence (to be planted *behind* the fence with instructions to grow through in case they were uprooted by the resident rascal), and yet another bag of nourishing puppy food; total bill £95. William was enjoying elite cuisine. My previous dog, Mischa had been delighted to have Tesco's own brand of dog food at £2.99 a packet supplemented with food scraps, but apparently growing puppies needed a complete diet with adjusted protein, calcium and energy levels, and all important vitamins and minerals at a cost of £11. If only Eukanuba would add some tasty tuna flakes then William would think he had arrived in gourmet heaven.

The only time William barked was for food or water. He gave his plaintive 'I am hungry' bark in the garden yesterday. Michael, my barn guest, had put out some bread on the patio table for the birds as there was a robin nesting in the ivy. William had hoovered up all the pieces he could reach on the edge of the table, leaving one piece he was unable to reach in the centre of the table, so he barked for assistance. I chatted to Michael and asked him kindly not to put bread there for the birds as William was being trained not to eat from the table.

The covered hose pipe presented a trickier problem. I looked at the complicated diagrams, counted thirty pieces to assemble and acted as feeble as a lettuce when Michael popped his head in. He took up the challenge and eventually, with a good deal of muttering and a certain amount of satisfaction, he pieced, pulled and screwed everything together. We tested it and it worked perfectly in preparation for William's next bath, so I immediately wheeled the hose out into a shed in the barn out of harm's way.

I visited the GP surgery again and saw my fifth (out of seven) sister, all of whom were lovely, kind and caring nurses, and we laughed as they squirmed at the sight of my mangled finger. I was comforted to see that it looked much healthier and thankfully less infected. The distal end of the nail was still hanging at a perilously jaunty angle but I clung on to it as we were rather attached. I was given appointments to have it dressed every other day and was most grateful for their care and concern.

Before the fourth Clicker Class William decided he had to have a crash course in behaving. He could sit, lie, stand, sit to order in any combination. He could respond to 'Come William' most of the time, he could come to the whistle at the speed of a lame tortoise, and he could walk happily to heel with his own style of variations such as round the heel and under the heel. Allowances had to be made for distractions such as flying geese (Canadian), barking dogs, rabbits and the odd noisy cockerel when things would go totally awry, and control would fly out of the window leaving William confused and me less confident of ever achieving my goal. If I wanted an obedient puppy I had to persist.

I asked Clicking Sally if there were any more intensive

classes for William and me to attend. Apparently there were only classes which train the trainers, but no classes which train with the click and reward system. When I reported that William had tugged Charlie's sleeve she said this was normal exuberant puppy behaviour, and that very young children should not play throwing games with puppies. She believed that this course of classes would train William to be an obedient pup.

In Class Four William learned to 'Wait, click and go for a treat' and also to 'Stay, click, receive a reward'. His party piece was an entirely self-designed performance. He lay belly down on the floor, legs akimbo, and imagined that no-one could see him, then he pee-ed whilst prone and watched the urine seeping out around him like the rivers of Babylon. There was no shame and no blame. Sally was astounded as she had never seen this happen before. However, I could not fail to notice that when Tracey or Sally wanted a puppy to demonstrate a new activity they side-lined William and chose a cute Springer or an obedient black and white Collie. His tricks were costing him dear. He was not going to be teacher's pet.

Nick came down to Devon to see the fierce, ferocious and thoroughly uncontrollable hound from hell. William was to prove him wrong. He turned into an affable, amiable and affectionate pussycat, lapping up all the stroking, fondling and cosseting on offer. They immediately bonded and became inseparable. The thought that Nick might whisk Wills off to Ireland without me was more than I could bear. William and I were a job lot; if one went to Ireland the other came too. Wills was anxious to show off his new-found skills by sitting, lying, and standing to order. He had more problems with waiting and staying, particularly when served chicken delicacies, but these were early days. He walked well to heel, but added a selection of moves of his own design to wrap the lead completely around Nick. They were great fun (both Nick and the dog) and we walked happily beside the River Taw thoroughly enjoying the 'take your puppy for a walk' experience. Miraculously, all weekend Wills performed all his bodily functions in the garden thus sparing the kitchen floor from further ritual onslaught. Nick was a happy bunny, I was a proud puppy owner and William basked in all the attention.

My hound from hell had spent the week chewing the new green plastic netting on the five-bar gate. He had made a William-sized hole so I spent a further £11 on the purchase of a roll of wire netting designed to confine persistently wayward animals, and gave Nick that all too familiar helpless look. He kindly removed the overly well-secured green plastic netting and stapled on the more robust replacement. The next morning I told Nick that the wind had been so gusty in the night that the netting had become detached from the gate and rolled itself back up. He gently explained that April 1st was the *next* day.

On Saturday afternoon Martin and Jo brought Martin's stepmother, Pat, and the children over for a Devon cream tea. William was confined to his pen for this short time in order to keep the children safe, and everyone seemed happy with this arrangement. Then in the night there was yet another gale. At 5.30am, as the wind blew with the force of a hurricane and the rain lashed against every window pane, I lay in bed thinking I cared not if William pee-ed over every inch of the kitchen floor with impunity, I was not, definitely not, venturing out in this inclement weather. I rose at 7.30am when a miracle happened: for the first time William sat by the door and whimpered to go out. Incredibly he went out alone, performed, and swiftly rushed back for his post-pee nuzzling and 'Good boy' congratulations. William was growing up to be a fine chap. I felt he was now ready for boarding school.

My cousin Claire's gifted daughter, Julia, had been granted a choral scholarship at The King's School, Ely, as a boarder. She was thrilled to have this amazing opportunity to sing in the beautiful cathedral and travel abroad with the Girls' Choir. I thought William ought to have every opportunity too. Whilst Julia was being trained to sing like an angel, William could be trained to behave like one. Nick gave me the telephone number of a gundog trainer, Sun Star Gundog Training, in Dorchester, Dorset, who was offering a three day course. Determined to steer my dog away from the gun, I looked on the web and found two other dog training schools, both of which offered three week courses and trained by the reward system. One of them, Royvon, owned by Roy and

Yvonne, no less, employed trainers who had trained the celebrities and their rescue dogs for the television programme 'The Underdog Show' hosted by Julian Clarey, which had made compulsive viewing. I was impressed. I immediately telephoned both of them to find out if I could accompany William. I left messages on both their answer-phones and waited patiently for a reply.

Meanwhile Walter Harrison from the Sun Star Gundog Training Centre telephoned back giving details of a three day course starting on May 5th , where I could board with William while learning how to train him to be obedient. Not all dogs who attended were destined to be gun dogs. The course cost £250. He gave me a pre-course tip that I should prevent William from having a ball in his toy box but take a tennis ball on each walk and throw it only twice. If he retrieved it, I was to stroke and make a great fuss of him. If he failed to live up to his name and retrieve, I was to ignore him. Walter was not a fan of treats or clickers, just cuddles and congratulations.

Which of these two training regimes would be best for William – and for me? I had to choose.

CHAPTER 5

THE PRICE OF PUPPY LOVE

WILLIAM HAD LIVED with me for seven weeks and his company had given me enormous pleasure. I was curious to discover the price of puppy love:

Dog bed, lead, toys, bowls, brush, treats, clippers	£100
Puppy pen (gift)	£165
One pedigree puppy (true cost £700) (gift)	£400
6 weeks of puppy food @ £11 per bag	£66
2 boxes of gravy bone biscuits	£4
Medical insurance	£199
Rabies injection and chip	£171
Clicker dog training	£50
Puppy shampoo	£6
Worm tablets	£5
Flea ointment	£5
3 weeks dog training course (gift)	£699.12
Plastic covered wire netting and posts	£25
Plastic netting for gate	£6
30 metre encased garden hose	£60
Wire netting for gate	£11
Slate over drinking trough	£40

Total to date   £2012.12

This worked out as £49 per day for 41 days of entertainment (discounting the day of the finger bite). I soon wished I had not totted up these expenses, it was a tad like counting the cost of a work of a precious work of art, or a sports car or even a priceless baby. I guess as the years roll by the daily cost will be substantially reduced. As an adult dog Mischa was very cheap to run with only two vet bills in her life, one for spaying and one when she was 12 years old and tragically contracted inoperable cancer of the spleen and sadly needed the vet's help at the end of her life.

I considered that William was ready for his first long journey. We travelled for two hours to visit my sister-in-law, Rosemary in Child Okeford who was entertaining my nephew's wife, Eve, and her two adorable daughters, Emily aged three-and-a-half years and baby Amber aged just three months. William threw up on the journey to Dorset so arrived not looking his best but soon recovered in time to enjoy a country walk negotiating stiles with convenient dog flaps and problem kissing gates which terminated by design at the Children's Playground for Emily. William was forbidden to enter the play area and sat patiently behind the fence and sulked. He wanted to be jumping and running with Emily as she dashed excitedly from one activity to another. During the walk he pulled to be with Emily and her new bright-coloured scooter (she insisted it had to be taken across the fields). He also eyed up a lady's two walking sticks and would have forced them from her if he had not been tightly reined.

He learned to sit on the pavement, instructed to look left and right and wait until commanded to cross the road when it was clear. He walked well to heel sometimes but was unable to decide which heel he preferred. I would have liked to say that he declined lunch but in fact he was not offered any to prevent a repeat bout of sickness on the return journey. I reminded myself that dogs in the wild had irregular meals, living with famine or feast according to the quarry killed. This solution worked well. Wills travelled home without spewing and more than made up for his missed meal by eating heartily when he reached home.

The brochure for the Sunstar Gundog Training Centre duly arrived. It provided details of a three day course at a cost of £250 for six month old dogs and novice handlers under the expert instruction of Walter Harrison, an international Field Trial Judge. Owners were taught how to handle their dogs in the shooting field in order to be prepared for the coming season. It covered steadiness, retrieving, teaching the dog to hunt close, steadying in the rabbit pen and water work. There was a large training pen where participants could hunt rabbits and there was also experience of dogging-in pheasants. Participants were required to bring two tennis balls (no problem), two dummies (where from?) and a whistle. Although Walter had indicated that the course was suitable for those who just needed obedience training and would not wish to hunt, I felt that the emphasis was strongly related to the shooting field and therefore not for me.

I was more intrigued by a special course for puppies from five to seven months of age organised by Royvon Dog Training in Merthyr Tydfil. There were three sessions, each lasting five days, at a combined cost of £595 + vat which could be tailor-made to fit in with work commitments. Retrievers were trained by a Retriever breeder and owners attended on the last day of each session to learn how to handle their now beautifully trained pets. They trained using the tested voice and praise method. No cruelty, no clickers and no reliance on treats. I was ambivalent about sending William away, but as I had to leave him anyway when I was lecturing, it made sense to let William enjoy some schooling while I was away working. I was particularly eager for him to learn to wait, stay and retrieve. I wondered if they could work their magic in these areas.

William kept his appointment at the vet's for a blood test three weeks after the anti-rabies injection. I lifted him out of the car but once on the ground he determinedly pulled me across the car park and in through the surgery door at a pace not befitting a lady of 66 years of age. Without a sideways glance at the receptionist he bounced unannounced straight in to the treatment room and met a delightful vet named Joss who was obviously an animal lover. She ruffled up his neck fur in sheer delight and William was in puppy heaven. She then proceeded to shave off a square of his precious fur in preparation for the blood test. Wills clearly objected to having his fur attacked but inevitably after two attempts offered up a full syringe of blood. He declined a treat in favour of further cosseting from Joss, begging her for more with his dreamy seal-like eyes and accepting this tactile reward like a man.

It was a prerequisite for the Royvon puppy training course for William to receive a kennel cough injection two weeks prior to attending so I booked this appointment for him. He was also popped on the scales (with a fair amount of difficulty) and weighed in at 20.5Kg, which fully explained why he felt like an elephant when I lifted him in and out of the car. Things had to change. He seemed to be doubling his weight every month. Very soon I would need a special vehicle with a hoist, a kind of pup-mobile.

I arrived home to find a cheque from Marks and Spencer covering William's bump aspiration bill which was settled in full with a credit of £30.98p. Perhaps Wills was starting to pull his weight. I imagined that he could be gainfully employed using those dreamy doe-eyes to pose for those appealing greetings cards, or failing that, he could be harnessed to a home-made trailer like the faithful hound of one of my back pain patients, whose pet pulled his golf clubs round the course for him and was the only dog allowed on the precious fairways.

I could just imagine William on a golf course building bunkers upon bunkers. Unsurprisingly when John the Builder arrived to dig a trench and lay a drainage pipe from my new conservatory, William volunteered to help. John left the lilac undisturbed, as agreed, sunk the pipe, fashioned a soak-away and neatly covered it over with soil. Later that afternoon William arrived back from the garden with his head completely covered in mud, soil and dust. This should have been predictable but I was unprepared. He had explored the newly turned soil and unearthed a brand new gleaming terracotta pipe. This boundless energy ought to be channelled into something useful like mining, tunnelling or even planting potatoes. 'Have puppy, will dig' could be the marketing slogan. My bumpy, bent tailed, balding bundle of delight could earn his keep.

Amid blue skies and glorious sunshine, my daughter, Claire arrived from London for the Easter break. True to form William became a bouncing jack-in-the-box. Unfortunately William's brain was still unable to control his bladder during raw excitement and he leaked in the kitchen for the first time in a week. I was glad that I had left the bucket and mop handy for such accidents. Both Claire and I asked him to sit each time he jumped up and he eventually calmed down and took his instructions like a well-trained hound. After lunch, Claire stripped off and lay on the lawn looking amazingly beautiful in her itzi-bitzi bikini. This was obviously more than William could handle for he pissed (Claire's word) all over her, her bikini and her matching sarong. Whether he was displaying his natural masculine superiority or was just excited to see her, Claire was deeply unimpressed. She shrieked, leapt up, and rushed inside to shower and change. At this stage William had not yet ventured on to the beach and I feared for the unsuspecting sun worshippers basking on the Devon sands.

I have been very twitchy about letting William roam free ever since I was walking my friends' dog in glorious countryside outside Quintin, Brittany, when disaster struck. Alphonse, Ann and John's beautiful beagle, had been taking himself for walks over the fields ever since his elderly owner had been too infirm to walk him. When his owner died, my friends gave him a wonderful home. Ann and I went for many walks with Alphonse and whilst we walked along the road and chatted, Alphonse would circle the fields often out of view and then suddenly appear ahead of us.

Last year, when Alphonse was geared up for a walk, Ann was delayed by a telephone call so I gestured that I would take him out. John gave me the lead and I took off. I met the local farmer who wagged his finger, indicating that Alphonse did not go for a walk on a lead. I released him and he took off exploring the fields. I walked in the same direction that Ann and I had walked the previous day. Suddenly I saw Alphonse rushing back to me from the strawberry fields on the other side of the road whilst at the same instant a car was approaching at speed round the bend. In a flash I could see what was going to happen. I waved to the car to slow down but the inevitable happened. There was a deadly thump as the car hit Alphonse and carried him 20 metres up the road. Then a shocked blood soaked Alphonse appeared from under the car walking slowly towards me. I thought he was going to die. There was blood coming out of his mouth and his left hind leg was cut to the bone. I stuttered some phrases in French asking the driver to take Alphonse and me back to my friends' house, and gave the necessary directions mostly by pointing furiously. We took Alphonse to the vet who diagnosed a full thickness laceration down the length of his left hind leg and a hole in his tongue where he had bitten clean through. Alphonse was swabbed, stapled together, prescribed antibiotics and equipped with an oversized lampshade. To my relief and delight he lived.

As I saw Alphonse hobbling around looking extremely sorry for himself I can remember thinking that I would rather that the accident had happened to my dog, not Ann and John's. I felt horribly responsible. I felt so low and eventually I returned home and collected Mischa. On arriving home she started drinking water incessantly, refusing her food and finding it an effort to move. She was also incontinent of urine. She had been perfectly well when I left, just stopping occasionally on walks to catch her breath like an elderly lady. She was 12 years old and had lived with me for the last eight years. I took her to the vet who diagnosed a tumour on her spleen which was so large that it could burst at any time and give untold pain. It was an awful shock. She told me gently that I did not have a choice as to what was the best for her. I anguished over the decision; it was a decision I could not make alone. After speaking to Claire and Nick I knew what was best for Mischa. I made the agonising decision to spare Mischa further suffering. I was bereft. I came home, tidied up Mischa's bed, bowls and effects, vacuumed the dog hair from the kitchen floor and when all was spick and span I sat down and howled.

To lose a dog was awful. There was no welcome, no faithful friend, no-one to eat the left over scraps and no-one to whom to open one's heart. I also missed our many and varied walks together. The house felt empty and unloved. Gradually over the next few months I came to terms with my loss and set my heart on a puppy, whom I hoped would grow up to be a beloved companion like Mischa.

Soon after the bikini incident, Claire's boyfriend, Neil arrived from Llandudno and we walked down the hill to the beautiful old stone bridge at Venn Quarry where it is compulsory for all my guests to tarry and play Pooh sticks. After

Claire claimed her (narrow) victory we took William under the stile and along the Tarka trail which followed the river upstream to Landkey. William was confined to an extending lead which provided much amusement every time he circled one of us and tied us up in knots.

William's first love was water: he could soak the kitchen floor just using his extra large paw and a water bowl; he could sit under a leaking gutter for hours letting the drips bounce on to his head in an attempt to catch a raindrop; his Christmases all came at once when he was sprinkled from the (pink) watering can; but the river provided truly the finest fascination of all time. With one jump he was in the fast flowing water up to his neck with an expression of pure ecstasy laced with a sprinkling of bewilderment and only surpassed by the sheer joyous pleasure obtained whilst shaking himself dry over his nearest and dearest. Entertainment value: priceless.

That evening Neil kindly lit a barbecue. We sensibly popped Wills in his play pen while cooking was in progress and extended this confinement while we were enjoying the al fresco cuisine. Afterwards, while the wine was still flowing, William was invited into his own garden. He smelt the aftermath of the steak and with sheer indignation to have missed the lion's share raced around the garden rattling the matches in his mouth before repeating the same exercise with the clotted cream. Since then he has added charcoal kindling wood to his self-styled diet of sticks, plant fibre, snail shells and rabbit pellets. Perhaps his nourishing puppy food was not so wonderfully balanced after all, if it lacked these vital ingredients.

On Easter Day Claire, Neil and I were invited to Martin and Jo's house for lunch. William was admitted to the garden and I was fearful for the survival of the tomato plants in grow bags, the herbs in pots and the seedlings that Martin had planted in neat rows in a new vegetable patch. Whether it was by design or just a quirk of fate but William decided to till the soil which was waiting to be planted. He doggedly dug holes which were large enough to plant giant root vegetables, albeit in a rather haphazard fashion. Martin was delighted to have a little husbandry assistance and I was relieved that no damage had been done (this time).

After lunch we visited Westward Ho! So it was with a certain amount of fear and trepidation that I let William off the lead for the first time on the beach. I knew he sometimes had a selective hearing problem when his name was called particularly if he was engrossed in a new and naughty activity. He made a bee-line for the sea. I was concerned in case he swam to Wales! However my worries were unfounded as he preferred to paddle along the water's edge, bouncing, jumping and splashing with all the boundless energy of an excitable young pup. Needless to say, he tucked in early that night from sheer exhaustion. A very contented puppy.

GROWING UP

SADLY I HAD to attend a funeral far from Devon which meant that William was packed off to stay with Carla for three days. Carla reported that William had settled down considerably since the last visit and had played well with three year old Jordan and her two young friends. He had stayed clean and dry with only two wet accidents in the kitchen. Carla had been dreading this visit ever since William's last stay when he was doubly incontinent and which she now admitted she had found extremely traumatic but this time there was a marked improvement now he was (almost) continent.

I needed four new tyres on my VW Golf so I took William to Rock Park in Barnstaple whilst they were fitted. This was a necessary expense as bald tyres could accrue six points on my driving license and one that even I could not cost out to William. I kept him on the lead but he tugged to speak to every man, woman and dog that walked past, walked near or indeed walked within sight. Needless to say the majority of people stopped and made a great fuss of him which only compounded the problem. Back at the tyre depot the staff gathered round and embraced him with their oily black fingers. I guess they treated him like a towel as he was a cleaner option than wiping their hands on their oily overalls. So with four brand new very expensive tyres we cruised home and I opened the car boot for William to jump out for the first time. He was getting too heavy to lift, so I waited and waited and eventually he made it. Another milestone in his short life. Next he needed to master the art of jumping in. And soon.

At four months old, William was still puppy-like with long gangling legs attached to extra large paws, the suggestion of curls to come and a madly cute expression. His black and dreamy eyes were responsible for many of his forays into naughtiness and beyond. He wanted to chase every moving thing irrespective of size from children to chickens, blackbirds to butterflies, and rivers to raindrops; all were attractive targets for a playful puppy with a large exploratory gene. He was madly curious, alert and totally prepared to explore the whole of Devon and its contents before embarking on a sight-seeing tour of the world. He was William the Inquisitive.

His large jet black nose was responsible for a totally different type of unsociable behaviour. He would roll in fox's faeces as soon as he was let off the lead, eat sheep droppings with the speed of a cheetah, and dig holes under the fence like a determined meerkat in an attempt to join the bouncing lambs in the adjoining field. He needed constant supervision, a large helping of patience and an armoury of distraction apparatus. Above all he was fun.

William adored attention. He was transported on to another planet when his neck was ruffled or his tummy stroked. His hairbrush was his best friend and he would present parts of his body in turn to be brushed and pampered, rolling over completely uninhibited with his lipstick fully erect. I would let the fur from the brush float away so that the birds could enjoy a fur lined nest but Wills had other ideas. He sprung like a playful kitten, and leapt like Nureyev performing a pas de quatre to reach his fluff and reclaim the balls of fur, which after all were his.

For William, sound was the most suspect of the five senses: taste, touch, sound, smell and touch. William could hear the gate catch click from the end of the garden, he cowered when the jets screeched past from Chivenor threatening to destroy my 500-year-old chimney stack and with it his delicate ear drums, he came running when I shook his biscuit box but failed to arrive when his name was called. I could not visit Saunton Sands calling 'William' and shaking his Pedigree gravy bones - or could I?

Taste was not a problem provided his breakfast, lunch and dinner were laced with tuna flakes or chicken titbits. He knew

Above: Frankie and William with their sister (Photograph by Glennis Hewitson)

Below: Grace with Mischa (Photograph by Mary Wilson)

Above: Julia at The King's School, Ely

Below: William in the garden

Above: Glennis showing Frankie (Photograph by Lesley Durrant)

Below: William

Above: Charlie, William and Maggie

Below: Charlie and William

not to beg at the table. The only time he barked was for food. He stayed silent when visitors arrived as a prelude to rolling over for a tummy tickle. He would allow workmen the freedom of the house. I wondered if I could train him to bark at intruders by using chicken-scented burglars.

I left William in his pen with a Kong filled with his favourite gravy bones to chew when I visited the University of the West of England, Bristol. When I arrived home I was delighted that his bladder had held out. With the speed of light I took him outside and made the mistake of congratulating him and giving him a tummy tickle whereupon from the incumbent position he directed a jet of pee over my trousers and shoes. Another lesson learned the hard way. It seemed that puppy training was always directed at the owners. 'Puppy behaviour' was normal. Owners had to learn not to give a pre-pee tickle, not to leave anything of value about, not to let children run around, and definitely not to remove lamb bones from a puppy's mouth. My finger was making good progress and, even though still bandaged in case the dead nail caught on anything, I was ignoring it. My calamity was deemed miniscule after I saw a horrendous photograph in the newspaper of a crocodile with his devoted keeper's severed arm in his mouth. Apparently surgeons performed a miracle and sewed the arm back on.

My friend Dorothy arrived from Surrey to spend some time with me in Devon. The weather was glorious even though it was still April. We took William to Instow and let him gallop across the beach where he joined two athletic young men playing football. Obviously my puppy preferred rugby to football. He became a one man team. He chased the ball with the speed of Jonas and when he intercepted it he scored a try. There were no goal posts, no conversion and for Wills no more play when we led a panting puppy away. We lunched at The Commodore and sat outside enjoying the view. We tied William to the table leg and had visions of him transporting the table across the patio, but he became a stationary star and positively purred to perfection when the formally-dressed waiter served him with a bowl of water from a silver jug.

Later, while Dorothy and I were chatting in the conservatory, William left the kitchen and came down the slate steps to join us. He adored Dorothy. Previously he had stayed put in the kitchen and I naively thought this rule would always apply. I shouted at him to go back to the kitchen whereupon he became totally confused and christened my new slate floor and sitting room carpet with a shower of pee. This experience taught me two lessons. Firstly, 'Close the kitchen door' and secondly, 'Do not shout'.

William has started to earn his keep. He was let out first thing into the garden and arrived back with a very dead mouse which he proceeded to bring into the kitchen. The pride on his face indicated that he was the culprit and I wondered what offering he would present to me next! Two days later he answered that question by bringing me another little recently expired mouse. The following night Michael walked out of the Barn in the dark for a smoke and trod on one of William's squeaky toys. He leapt in the air in shock. He thought he had killed a kitten. Although William was wont to scatter his toys around, his retriever skills were developing apace. He could respond to 'Fetch', 'Come William' and 'Drop' when I threw balls for him. His 'pièce de resistance' was to hold two tennis balls in his mouth at a time rather resembling an overgrown hamster.

Dorothy came with me to Click Class Six purely for the entertainment value. A miracle happened. William enjoyed showing off. He could have been on the stage. A beautiful young helper named Zaina asked me to demonstrate 'Sit, Down, Sit, Stand' and also 'Sit, Wait and Come William' routine. Wills obeyed every command and received copious congratulations. Zaina said he was excellent which was the ultimate praise. I had asked Wills to 'Sit and Wait' before every bowl of food and this training had eventually paid off. Sally asked him to walk to heel. I had a show dog with no problem there. I did mention to Sally that in the real world William pulled and I had trouble holding him when my arm left its socket. She kindly gave me a nose straining halter to try out. Tracey asked us to demonstrate 'Sit, Stay' whilst I turned and walked away and to my amazement Wills stayed still and came to me on the command 'Come William'. He was word perfect. I left the class on a high believing for the very first time that I was going to have an obedient dog.

Dorothy asked me why I should ever require William to 'Stay'. I mentioned that Nick had seen black flat-coated retrievers in the open tailgate of Range Rovers staying obediently whilst their master was salmon fishing until commanded to 'Come'. I replied that it would be useful to be able to control a dog so that it would stay. Whereupon Dorothy replied: "Surely you're not going to leave your boot open in Barnstaple car park and expect William to stay put!".

At the class we were warned of the hazards of certain foods by Tracey who grimly illustrated the point by telling us about an unfortunate dog who had tragically died after eating a Mars bar. We were also given a guide listing 208 poisonous plants alphabetically from Aconite to Yew that were toxic or fatal to dogs and which included many plants whose common name was unknown to me let alone the botanical term. William had made sure this was not a problem for us by uprooting most of the garden with his fast developing network of tunnels. We were also given a handout on Digging. The leaflet advised owners to allow their dogs somewhere, preferably on the beach. If this failed, they should purchase a sand pit for the persistent digger. As a last resort, they should concrete over the garden! Wise words, but concreting over half an acre would be a bit excessive!

As we left William's school we met Rex, a male Retriever from the next class who was also four months old. He was half the size of my beautiful brute. Was he missing out on expensive puppy nuts with the necessary supplements? Was he anorexic? Had he been smoking? In comparison I had a monster puppy who was going to dwarf his parents and become a veritable giant. Did he have an overactive pituitary gland? Perhaps Crufts had a 'Biggest in Breed' section for Retrievers. Why, he could win cups just for size! He was not obese, just big. I took Big Willy home and measured him; from the bump on his head to the floor he stood 27 inches high, from the tip of his black nose to the end of his now curly tail he was 52 inches long. His bushy tail was an alarming 17 inches in length and his front paws were 3 inches wide and built like shovels. He then rewarded me for my interest by departing with the tape measure!

He took my tape measure to the tunnels under the Barn

which had now joined up and buried it. If the walls had not been three feet thick I am sure the ancient building would have caved in. Perhaps my mammoth pup was hell bent on living life below the Barn in a self-constructed capacious cave like a hound's hideaway or even a bargain basement. Perhaps he was measuring up.

I took my overgrown pup for a walk wearing his recently borrowed halter. I always thought that hounds wearing a nose strap were muzzled and prone to bite. I did not wish the world to know that William was prone to the odd finger. William was not a biter (I was confident of that now that my finger had healed and was exposed to the air albeit with only half a finger nail). William took an instant dislike to the halter. He hated it. He spent most of the time trying to remove the black nose strap with his rather large furry paws. When this failed he lay down doggo refusing to move before plaintively showing me the whites of his sad eyes. Certainly this halter prevented him from pulling but now it was me who was doing the tugging, not him. I did not want to pull his head off. I despaired.

William and I went to the vet's to see Joss. My now adolescent puppy bounded in at alarming speed with me flying behind him like a distraught overweight Mary Poppins. He adored Joss who rewarded him with a phial of live kennel cough vaccine up the left nostril followed by a couple of his customary treats (in his mouth). Life was good. It was exactly two weeks before my puppy would be kitted out for boarding school and this vaccine was one of the compulsory requirements. At least I was spared sewing on name tapes. Joss warned me that William might develop a cough in two or three days time. I paid £18.84 for the privilege and wondered how you coped with a coughing puppy. Perhaps he ought to have some Vic rub and dog sized tissues in his pen or maybe some company was producing puppy linctus potions. Whilst I was there I stocked up with a large bag of Hill's chicken flavoured food designed for the largest size of puppy. I enquired about William's blood test results which apparently were still locked in the laboratory. On arriving home I found a message for me to make another vet appointment to collect William Dorey's passport as he had passed his anti-rabies blood test with flying colours. In six months time he could spread his legs and travel the world. Was the world ready for William?

As it was a lovely day I took Wills to the Millennium Green where he met Tember (born in September), a tiny black Labrador puppy. They jumped over each other in turn and tumbled their way round the park keeping nose to tail in a variety of interesting combinations until they finished up rolling together into a muddy ditch. Both dogs disappeared from view. My darling champagne coloured dog changed to black in an instant, whereas Tember seemed totally unchanged. I led William to the river to rinse but to no avail. The ditch proved much more fun. I dragged him back to the car and lifted this foul-smelling animal into the boot before hosing him thoroughly at home and watching the diluted Millennium mud gush down the drive. The joys of having a mucky mutt were replaced by the delights of doggy-scented wet fur. Not the best smell in the world.

The next day my friend and student Kay arrived from Harrow-on-the -Hill for a week to concentrate on her PhD studies and to meet my new puppy. She was totally entranced by my daft mutt. As it was a glorious day we drove to Croyde and walked through the safe pathway to the beach. Some passers by ignored William, but most were delighted to see a young puppy and stopped to stroke and fondle him. You could tell immediately who were the ardent dog lovers. Wills, however, was not that bright. He believed that everyone was capable of giving him attention and was peeved when he was ignored. He desperately craved attention from all humans, unless of course there was a dog around. Then his loyalty changed and he gave his full attention to those on four legs; the friskier, the better.

On the beach he loped up to two tiny children in swimsuits who were digging in a deep sand bunker so that only their heads were visible. When they saw a huge hound making for them they ran away in panic. "Stand still!" I shrieked. "Don't move or he'll chase you!" I yelled. Fortunately they obeyed and froze in terror while I captured my excitable puppy and offered profuse apologies.

William paddled along the waters edge with sheer joy and

wonderment, avoiding each wave as it threatened to lap his large paws, but this delight was surpassed by the supreme ecstasy of digging in the wet sand. And not just digging. He choreographed his own particular brand of nosing, rolling and writhing movements for his beach dance. He became completely caked in sand, a living sand sculpture clearly in need of a high pressure hose. I was aware that we were going straight to Click Club Seven and wished to arrive relatively sand free. We led him to the stream and requested a river dance. The pirouetting stopped. He paddled happily but resolutely refused to bathe, splash or rinse.

I took my sandy puppy to class. Kay had never been to Obedience Dog Training before and was intrigued by the smartly organised outfit and enthusiastic tutors. She became thoroughly entertained by all the puppies and their adoring owners. William was the largest pup there and disappointingly failed to display the same excellence as he had done the previous week. When Sally asked him to go 'Down', he refused and I (rather unfairly) received the blame. I had always indicated with my hand that Wills should lie down and this seemed to work, but now I was expected only to command without gesticulating.

Tracey talked to us about castration. William instinctively placed his paws over his ears. She heartily agreed with castration. I winced for Wills. The perils of non-castration were plentiful. We were warned not to use our dogs for stud, as once they had enjoyed the pleasures and joys of mating they would leave home and often travel miles to seek a bitch on heat. Tracey felt there were too many dogs in the world, judging by the number needing to be rescued. Whole dogs were liable to have prostate problems. Whole dogs cocked their legs and scent-marked. I listened to the case for castration and was unconvinced. There was no case against. Glennis, my friend the breeder, never has her dogs castrated and has never had problems with any of them. Nick was adamant that Wills should be intact. His dogs had balls. I thought I would ask the vet next month at William's free six month check up.

CHAPTER 7

OFF TO BOOT CAMP

W E WERE GIVEN the next week off from puppy
school as it was the May Bank Holiday, and invited
to appear for our last session two weeks later with
a well-rehearsed trick such as proffering a paw, rolling over or
presumably presenting a full song and dance act. It was a
great relief that William would be at Boot Camp (his training
course in Wales) at that time so we were spared the effort of
practising and performing a routine. I had no idea what we
would have conjured up. William's forte was connected
strongly to digging, mouse catching, and muck rolling, none
of which would delight the assembled class. I wrote a letter to
Tracey and Sally thanking them for all their expert tuition and
marvelled at the way a five month old puppy could behave
following their skilled guidance. I then popped the clicker in
a drawer.

5th May 2007

Dear Tracey and Sally

*I would like to thank you for your kindness and patience in
helping to train young William. I am amazed how much we
have achieved to date thanks to your expert guidance. We will
continue our daily practice sessions. I am full of admiration for
all your good work and would be interested to receive details of
the advanced class.*

*I am sorry that due to work commitments I am sadly unable to
attend the last training session which includes the demonstration of a trick. William would have performed an accomplished*

high jump clearing a three foot bar followed by a forward roll and curtsey!

With best wishes

Grace Dorey

As William was going to miss his debut as a circus performer I was curious to see if I could train him to perform a party trick. So armed with a 50p bag of tasty morsels from the Click and Liver Club I proceeded to train my not-so-little miracle. I placed two watering cans on the newly mown lawn: the galvanised one with the hole in the bottom and its pretty pink replacement. I found a long stick and straddled it across them. I then proceeded to train my hound to jump by leaping over it myself with a complete lack of finesse. The commands used were 'William sit', 'Wait' and 'Come William'. After a few tries Wills was perfect and ready to have an audience so we proudly demonstrated William's newly acquired skills to a disbelieving Kay. There was no roll of drums but William sat, waited and came smartly to my side around the *outside* of the pink watering can. Kay and I collapsed with laughter. It was raw comedy. William looked sufficiently embarrassed and slunk away. No jump, no praise and no liver. Not wishing my puppy to be an abject failure, we tried again. This time he performed a perfect jump, easily clearing the stick, and received an Olympic sized ovation. I could just imagine William's stick trick at Click Eight: I would have to explain to the assembled group that William would first go over the bar, then around it, but not necessarily in that order! The next day it was time to raise the bar and go for gold.

In fact the next day William was busy as he had to collect his royal blue Passport from Katya, enabling him to come back into the UK any time after October 5th 2007. He would be welcomed back into the country provided he received the obligatory anti-tick treatment and echinococcus tapeworm treatment 24 to 48 hours before travelling home. His chip was scanned and found still to be in place between his shoulder blades, and he weighed in at 24.5Kg the weight of a fully grown hippopotamus. On arriving home from the vets he was encouraged to perform his new trick. Each time he went round the side of the pole. Was this due to a razor-sharp mind or did he really not have a clue? Or was he above this nonsense now he was a proud European passport holder?

Later that day Kay and I took William on a beautiful walk along the river Taw from Venn to Bishops Tawton, following the trail taken by Tarka the Otter. It was May 4th and the most glorious day of the year. Indeed it was a cloudless day with the bluest of blue skies. Life was good and the scenery exquisite. Progress was fine until we came to a field of curious young bullocks. They met us at a stile and frighteningly increased in numbers until the whole herd had assembled and dared us to pass. They stared menacingly. Wills barked incessantly whilst their curiosity increased exponentially. We took stock of the situation and beat a hasty retreat. We climbed up a hill carefully skirting a field of rape to join the road, rather than risk being trampled to death by the inquisitive herd. In the sunshine William began to wilt and needed to be cajoled to reach our destination where he was able to quench his thirst.

We lunched under a sunshade at the Chichester Arms where William met an eight- year-old female Retriever belonging to a retired couple from Spain who were happily holidaying in Devon. They commented on William's size and categorically emphasized that I would be unable to hold him when he grew larger if he took a fancy to a rabbit or squirrel. They suggested a chest harness which apparently placed pressure on the front legs. This seemed a better alternative to the nose strap and in need of investigation.

As it was so hot we decided to take the bus home. Fortunately there were no steps to board the bus so William walked happily on without a problem. William's ticket cost 20p. He enjoyed his bargain ride which was made special by copious attention from the other passengers. I mused that he would be a happier bunny if I exchanged my VW Golf for a bus. We alighted at Newport and started the journey uphill to Portmore. Kay went ahead as she had to collect her boyfriend from Tiverton Station and was running late. In the heat William started panting; he then pulled me across the road to the shade where he collapsed on a grassy bank. He refused to move. His panting increased and his breathing became more laboured. I sat there for ages stroking him. I was worried he might have a heart attack. I had no telephone, no purse and no way of summoning help. Eventually a thoughtful lady named Kate stopped her car and asked if we were all right. I replied that William had collapsed in the heat, and she kindly gave us a lift back home in the back of her car. I thanked her for being such an angel. William tumbled out of the car and hastily replaced his fluid deficit before falling fast asleep.

That evening while I was having dinner out with my friend Jennie, a sex counsellor (colleague) and great fun, Kay and her handsome boyfriend Paul agreed to look after the exhausted William. While they were sipping champagne, he (William not Paul) recovered sufficiently to burrow into the middle of the lawn, catch Mouse No. 3 and ruin Kay's Christian Dior sunglasses costing £200. His pre-bedtime wild skirmishes were not diminishing. Was this how dogs behaved in the wild? When would he calm down?

He was improving in one vital area. During the week that Kay stayed with me there were no puddles or worse in the kitchen. William's five month old bladder and brain were now working synergistically to store urine until the appropriate time and place for urination. He could now hold on from 9pm to 7.30am which was far better than I could manage. One morning whilst Kay was showering and occupying the bathroom I took Wills out for his early morning pee when my own first call to empty my bladder became too urgent to suppress. I squatted down behind my Barn at the exact time that my neighbour was passing my gate with a shotgun over one shoulder and a fox held aloft in the other hand! What worried me was that he passed by unflinchingly as if this al fresco peeing was a normal practice in the countryside. After breakfast William poo-ed outside (alone) when his gastro-colic reflex worked a treat. He used a variety of dumping grounds and afterwards I had to search the garden for the novel places he used in order to keep my barren garden turd-free. Even more importantly he performed these functions in the garden without me acting as chaperone and quality controller. I was delighted and the kitchen started smelling of roses.

On a bright day in early May, I took my bladder and bowel trained student to his boarding school at Merthyr Tidfil. He survived the journey with no accidents at either end (just a little light slobber). He was warmly received and we said our goodbyes and he was taken to his pen. I was given his lead and bade farewell. I found this very emotional as it conjured up memories of being given back the lead after dear Mischa was euthanised. I shed a tear. And then a few more.

I had packed my monthly work commitments into these five days. During this time I treated patients in Harley Street, ran a Study Day for Chartered Physiotherapists Promoting Continence on SS Great Britain in Bristol, trained a nurse into the protocol of pelvic floor exercises for a multi-centre government-funded post-prostatectomy trial, and delivered two lectures at the Association for Continence Advice Conference in Manchester, then supervised a PhD student in Bristol. Throughout this programme of work I worried incessantly about William. I missed him.

On the train I read books about other wayward hounds. There was no hope for me! I became a sad, single, dog book anorak. I found myself totally obsessed by the positive or negative experience of other dog owners. I preferred those at the negative end of the spectrum. They made Wills seem angelic in comparison. I found 'Walking Ollie' by Stephen Foster to be a delightful story of a wilful rescue dog whose character was paternally predetermined and I identified with him strongly. I found 'From Baghdad, with Love' by Jay Kopelman to be a most moving account of the rescue of a beloved dog named Lava from the dangerous military war zone. If only the same energy had been given to getting our troops safely home. I read 'Buster's Secret Diaries' by Roy Hattersley, which gives an insight into the world and his owner from the dog's point of view, though judging by the scant size of this book, Buster had probably buried some pages of his diary in a long forgotten spot. The week before, I had read 'The Curious Incident of the Dog in the Night-Time' by Mark Haddon, which gives a most moving account of a plucky boy with autism who played detective against all odds to identify who had killed a much-loved dog with a pitchfork.

I had previously read 'Marley and Me' by John Grogan,

which must rank above all as a classic tale of the life and upbringing of an unpredictable Labrador and must have given rise to a rash of dogs named Marley. Indeed there was one Retriever similarly named at the Click and Lick Club. Subsequently, I was sent 'Flush' by Virginia Woolf which tells the illuminating story of Elizabeth Barrett's devoted cocker spaniel living in privileged society in the nineteenth century, a dog who sat devotedly at her feet on her day sofa for five years while she was recovering from the trauma associated with the loss of her favourite brother. I have since scoured the internet for similarly entertaining books and have purchased from Amazon 'Copper: A Dog's Life' by Annabel Goldsmith, which portrays the life of a clever and cunning cross-bred (not mongrel) dog, who used to wait for the electric gates to open, then slip out, crossing main roads at the traffic lights for a walk in the park, finishing up with a visit to the pub where he was regularly lifted on to a bar stool as a local hero. The more I read about other dogs the more I missed young William. I was also concerned that he might be pining too.

I need not have worried, William was in good hands. Back in Wales, I met Gwyneth, the trainer who clearly adored William. She judged Retrievers and repeatedly enthused about my lovely dog. She asked to view his pedigree (see appendix) and was very impressed with his genealogy. With such exemplary breeding, could William deliver? William bounded out of his kennel and promptly pee-ed over my shoes in his excitement at seeing me. He lay down whilst I ruffled up his silky recently shampooed fur, nuzzled him behind his ears, cuddled his neck and rubbed his growing tummy. His stomach was not the only part that had grown. His lipstick became a glistening raspberry ice lolly standing proud from its wrapping. I averted my gaze out of mock modesty when Gwyneth kindly remarked: "He looks very pleased to see you!".

I was taken to a large indoor arena where I was given a demonstration of exemplary 'heel walking' with a limp lead, 'Sit, stay and recall' and 'Staying down'. What more does a girl want? What was the secret? It seemed as if there were two important training tools. One was a pouch full of chopped Co-op chipolatas and the other a choke chain. I shuddered at the thought of Wills having a choke chain after Click Tracey had explained that a vet had recently examined the brains at post mortem of dogs whose owners had used choke chains. He found there was evidence of brain damage in these dogs compared with dogs tethered to normal leads. This raised another research question. Were the dogs placed on choke chains because they were uncontrollable, wilful or just plain scatty? This would have totally skewed the research. This research should have had similar subjects randomised into either a choke chain group or a control group.

Gwyneth showed me how the training choke chain worked. There was never a large tug, just gentle tweaks if William strayed from heel position whilst undergoing obedience training. This was accompanied by a sing song 'Ah Ah' in Welsh if he strayed. I was given a pocket full of chipolata cubes, thanked M&S that my jacket was washable, and proceeded to emulate the expert. William was position perfect. I was impressed and wondered if he would still stay focussed in the company of other dogs. A Spaniel named Lola was brought into the training area. Gwyneth explained that she would not use the female Retriever whom William was caught humping on the day of his arrival, when they were put in the same pen together for company! No wonder he had enjoyed his stay. Was William intending to spread his pedigree genes all over Wales? Would he flatten the Spaniel?

William gave a charmed performance in front of Lola when led by Gwyneth and later by me. He held his head high as if to demonstrate that he was descended from a long line of Champions. In the ring, dogs are shown using a slip chain high under the head to encourage fine deportment and superior carriage. William was a star. I thanked Gwyneth profusely, booked his next five-day training in a month's time, and walked smartly towards my car. Suddenly William pulled me sideways in an effort to return to his pen. He wanted to stay.

Anxious to put our expensive Welsh training to good use, Wills and I set off for the Millennium Green. I still had to lift my clever mutt into the car but now at least he jumped out on cue. I walked him round the Green, sans sausages, but using little tweaks of the choke chain accompanied by a few too many Welsh 'Ah Ahs'. A man sitting on a bench, patiently waiting for his missing dog to return, commented: "He is walking much better than my dog". I said he was a five month old puppy in training and he replied: "If he grows much bigger, you will be able to ride him round!". My monster puppy walked splendidly all round the Green until he was 100 yards from the car, when he lay down and stayed down. No cajoling would move him. I wanted to telephone Gwyneth. I could not give the borrowed choke chain a yank so I waited. And waited. This should have been a frankfurter moment. I had a pocket full of dry treats which were spurned. I carried him into the car and headed for Tescos.

John, my neighbour living opposite, who has just been given the second transplant of a living beating heart in the country (and the first from Harefield Hospital), popped across to discuss having our chimneys rendered rainproof. William jumped up at the gate while John let himself in. I gave the command 'Down' and instantly the obedient William lay down - taking John's track suit bottoms with him! This resulted in an indignant neighbour with a chilly back-side while I tried desperately to conceal, if not completely contain, my uncontrolled mirth. William had at last found a party trick with promising potential.

CHAPTER 8

PLAYMATES

I WAS EAGER to compare my clever puppy with his brother so I invited Glennis and William's littermate, Frankie, for afternoon tea. Frankie was about three inches taller, much rounder, with a stronger head, the same size ten feet and smooth thick fur, paler than William's, but with not a curl in sight. I thought William was large but he was dwarfed by his sibling who, I was told, was already taller than their father at only five months old. Frankie was not trained to sit or lie down as he was destined for a career standing in the show ring, hopefully culminating in being shown at Crufts.

Even though he was slighter, my curly-furred puppy played top dog and tried to dominate his brother at every opportunity and beyond. This may have been because they were playing in his hallowed and holy garden, or it may have been due to his over assertive, nay bossy, nature. They rolled around in every conceivable position so that legs, ears and tails flew in all directions making it difficult to identify whose flailing appendage belonged to whom, but when the music stopped they always landed up with William on top. In the wild this play fighting would have served as training in the selection process for the dominant alpha male. I had been told that I had the quiet docile male in the litter. Had the pups been switched and had I mistakenly collected the dominator? Frankie was destined to become a Champion Retriever whilst I owned William the Conqueror.

William was up for another conquest. I was lecturing on erectile dysfunction to a wonderful group of physiotherapists who care for the elderly (over Seventies - phew, not there yet!)

in Plymouth, and left Wills with Carla for the night. I could not sleep. I hated being in the house on my own and no sooner had I left William and his tackle at Carla's house than I started to miss him. The house seemed empty and unloved. There was no cute friend waiting to eagerly welcome me in the morning, no-one to share the deafening screeching cacophony of sound that is described poetically as 'the dawn chorus', and no cute puppy lying on his back providing his special recipe of mouth-watering unconditional love. I missed my monster. When I came home from Plymouth I rushed round to collect my treasured pet and came face to face with a grubby mutt. His sensuous soft silky cream fur was replaced by a crispy brindled black and grey coat flecked with brown and spattered with mud as he had apparently spent the day rolling around the garden in joyous delight with Sky. That posed no problem as dry mud brushed off well and there was plenty of puppy and kitten shampoo available for the muckiest of pups.

While Carla was getting William's effects together I asked her sweet little four- year-old daughter, Jordan, if William had enjoyed himself. "Oh yes," she remarked. "William had a lovely time riding Sky." Carla came out and corrected Jordan: "No Jordan, not riding Sky, tiring Sky," to which Jordan replied: "No Mummy, William was riding her and pushing her along!" He came home and slept; he was seriously shot to pieces. These conquests were demanding.

William's cavalier attitude was also evident at home. If his motto was 'Conquer and Collapse', his heraldic coat of arms would portray a shield with a talbot (hunting dog) rampant sinister facing a talbot couchant (knackered) dexter both wearing a triumphal laurel crown but with unfettered collars to signify freedom. Below the crest would be a maze of undy (wavy) tunnels with eradicated (uprooted) plants.

William expressed this new found freedom by squeezing through the previously pooch-proof plastic coated wire fence in an effort to remove the labels from the new and up till now flourishing lavateria plants before rearranging their foliage just as they were happily bursting into bloom. He removed their vital support sticks and presented the colourful labels and chewed up stakes at my kitchen door. I was not amused.

The flowering shrubs had been planted the other side of the fence for their protection, now even they were unsafe. No plant was spared. My self-seeded poppies were flattened. The lawn suffered silently and now sported enough bunkers to grace a full-sized golf course. The underground passages were increasing in length, depth and width, aided by a few canine pals who came to visit and were only too keen to learn excavation skills from a master burrower. William had shown Sky how to dig. Between them they dug deep down under Carla's fence with determination reminiscent of The Great Escape or in William's case to visit the Alsation bitch living next door.

I now had a skilled hound who was eminently employable and able to earn his keep in a number of eclectic ways. He could be hired out as a vermin exterminator (mice only), trouser remover (men only to date), bunker designer or champion digger. His crested curriculum vitae complete with his full pedigree name 'Seruilia Snowball' sired by 'Gatchells Lone Ranger' with 'Bedeslea Blushing Bride Via Seruilia' as the dam (how do breeders conjure up such obscure names?) was extraordinarily impressive and beginning to render him eminently marketable. Whilst his brother Frankie ('Seruilia Snowbear') sold his soul to the show ring, William would be hard at it earning an honest crust and keeping his mind away from his true calling of becoming an unpaid stud to all the bitches in Barnstaple. Obviously this vocation came from his maternal grandfather, the Seruilia stud 'Steamroller Stan'! Wills had an exemplary pedigree and diverse practical skills but there was no getting away from it: 'Snowball' had stonking bonking genes.

I visited a Garden Centre on my way back from consulting at The Somerset Nuffield Hospital in Taunton, with a view to purchasing some heavyweight pet-proof netting. The only thing I could find that was at all suitable was a rabbit pen with eight wire panels flat-packed, forming a stylish hexagonal-shaped bunny run. The panels were the right size for my needs and seemed sturdy enough for the wildest member of the family Leporidae (rabbits and hares) so I brought them home to spread them out along the fence that William had penetrated. The only trouble was that the hinges were designed at an obtuse angle and the panels refused to lie straight. I did my best, which was fairly inadequate, muttered and mumbled a little too profusely and waited for Barry, my gardener, to arrive and staple the panels to the fence posts. I think he was amused at my wish to fashion a rabbitry into a fortified fence but he tactfully said nothing and set to work. He surveyed the flattened lavateria and declared that it would live (phew!) but guessed that the poppies had been chewed from their stalks by rabbits, chickens or some other hungry unnamed creature. This incident showed that one tended to blame the hardened criminals first when faced with a new and unsolved crime. I had blamed William rather unfairly for the poppies' demise and now was curious to find the culprit. There was no joy in waiting for the mysterious muncher or phantom pecker to re-offend as there was not one poppy to patrol (and it was raining).

Puppies seem to chew anything and everything with no respect for treasured possessions or property. It is impossible to watch them every moment and there has to be a gradual build-up of trust. Sometimes the damage William did was plain maddening but sometimes it was maddeningly expensive. Over the last nine years I have looked after a number of Glennis's dogs when she has been on holiday or away judging dog shows and they have, to date, ruined one walking boot, one vacuum cleaner nozzle, one hosepipe nozzle, one sheepskin hat (Christmas wrapped), two theatre tickets (in the sheepskin hat) and my daughter's cheque book. The theatre tickets still managed somehow to gain admission from a dog loving usherette with a warped sense of humour and Claire was rather proud of her dog-eared cheques. The other items had to be replaced.

William was quite capable of inflicting this amount of damage in one afternoon if such items were left within reach. Things could have been worse. While Wills was gaily disrupting the lavateria his brother Frankie was busily chewing through the outlet pipe to Glennis's washing machine, a felony which became extremely evident during the pumping and emptying cycle when soapy water and suds gushed out all over the kitchen floor and down to the sea. It became patently obvious who was responsible for this misdemeanour when the plumber (an obvious Sherlock Holmes fan) glee-fully showed her the offending hose which was peppered with multiple bite marks.

Dental misdemeanours aside, William was well prepared for the next term at his Welsh academy where he would see his friend and tutor Gwyneth. He had fulfilled his commit-ment to walk to sausage round the park and could 'Sit' and 'Wait' expectantly before every meal until he was given per-mission to eat. However, he was still jumping up excitedly when every visitor arrived and unsurprisingly many folk who disliked dogs were not happy with this behaviour which was even unpleasant for those who loved puppies. On hind legs he towered over me rather frighteningly, resembling a performing stallion, so he needed further lessons in respond-ing to the 'Down' command particularly when he was over excited.

William had somehow attained his first half birthday, turning six months old on June 6th. In human years he would now be three-and-a-half years of age (dog age times seven), a similar age to my grand-daughter Charlie who had emerged delightfully from the terrible twos and was now thoroughly enjoying the thrilling threes but still in need of adult guid-ance and a kindly kindergarten.

As part of his celebrations I took my adorable monster to the vet's for a free check up. I think Wills was lucky to be seen by a male vet because Robert made no mention of castration. Not a whisper. I had been told by Katya that this would be discussed at the six months check up so either Robert was uncomfortable broaching the subject or he simply forgot. Both Wills and I remained tacit; I not wishing to bring up this sen-sitive subject in front of my loveable monster and William wanting to hang on to his balls. Either way my growing pup may not have heard because Robert found a build up of wax in his ears, which may have gone some way to explain his selective hearing. Robert prescribed him some ear lotion, some more worm powder and some anti flea and tick lotion for good measure. Our 'free' appointment cost £36.51p. Clever, eh!

Two young men came to scale my 500-year-old chimney in order to cure the dampness creeping down my cob bedroom wall every time it rained. They took glorious photographs of the Devon countryside from this elevated position. While one of these kind men, Dave, was walking round my grass bank to the ladder in front of my cottage he was unfortunately bitten on the calf by Max, an Airedale who belonged to the holiday makers in my Barn. They were distraught. Fortunately Dave was wearing trousers and the injury had not drawn blood, but there were purple bruises corresponding to violent pressure from each of Max's teeth. Dave was remarkably stoic and good-natured about this catastrophe and announced he would proudly show his wounds to his mates in the pub that night. As a way of reassuring Dave that these things do happen, I told him about my window cleaner who arrived one day and dropped his trousers (because I was medical) and showed me the deep teeth marks from an Alsation who had punctured his bottom. These events showed me yet again the enormous responsibility of being a dog owner, and I was greatly relieved that William was not the perpetrator.

Nick kindly whisked me off to Hotel Sacher in Vienna for five days while he (William not Nick) was being trained and we departed most conveniently from Cardiff Airport, a stone's throw from the dog college at Merthyr Tidfil. I delivered my clean-eared, worm and flea free dog to training camp where he rushed in with the speed and determination of a rutting stag. I then spent a glorious few days in Vienna with Nick visiting all the known spectacular sights and admiring the exquisitely beautiful Austrian architecture. I had always wanted to visit this fairytale city and now my dream was coming true. We were fortunate to have tickets for a performance of the Spanish Riding School featuring the elegant and expertly trained Lipizzaner stallions. These horses are born as black foals but their coats amazingly change to pure white when they are four years old. It takes eight years to train these magnificent creatures to perform their choreographed ballet and at times stand elegantly on hind legs. Could William learn the opposite manoeuvre in just five days?

The Lipizzaner Horses were all they were cracked up to be and were surpassed only by the performance of two amorous very furry black bears in the Schloss Schönbrunn Summer

Palace Zoo who were spending the afternoon contentedly coupled together, completely oblivious to the curious audience they had attracted. The excessive heat, which must have been close to 30 degrees Centigrade, did nothing to quell their prolonged passion. Throughout this break every time I saw an animal, or more particularly a dog or a picture of a dog of whatever size, shape or breed, I missed William. We also visited the world famous Pathologisch-Anatomisches Bundesmuseum, and among the many models and photographs displaying unfortunate and often gross genetic malformations of nature we saw a photograph of a man with two penises. Gosh! William had enough trouble with one.

When I returned to Royvon Training School, William rushed up to meet me before lying down and excitedly losing bladder control yet again. This was becoming the norm and I kept my shoes well away from his outpouring of love and urine. During his stay William had changed colour. He now sported a green backside and green legs. The kennels had been painted in a non-marking paint, which appeared to defy trade-description legislation and every canine convention. Then Nick and I watched Gwyneth walk the colourful William to heel (and chipolata) and instruct him to sit, lie down and stay with complete success. I was able to copy Gwyneth and a willing William performed beautifully for me. He clearly enjoyed all the attention, adored Gwyneth and my green legged hound gave a class performance. What a star! He was rewarded with a shampoo in the Grooming Parlour before embarking on the long journey to Devon.

On reaching home I heard from Glennis that Frankie, William's sibling, had won first prize in the puppy class of a dog show in Cornwall, the first show he had entered. To me this was not unexpected as he was a fine dog destined for stardom. What a family of troupers!

William was pleased to find that my new Barn holidaymakers had a stunning two year old female russet Retriever named Mia. William was like a dog with two tails. All his Christmases had come at once. He bounced, flounced and pounced excitedly expecting this new playmate to run and roll with him in wondrous delight culminating in a free ride or two. However, his pre-coital posturing was instantly spurned by Mia who gave a series of shrill and rather startled barks that completely knocked his socks off, and every time he came close she ran smartly away as fast as her shapely legs could carry her. Mia had been spayed and was clearly not interested in this amorous cavorting and from then on, whenever Wills was on the prowl, she hid either in the car or deep inside the Barn. She cleverly secured a position of safety by somehow ascending the spiral staircase and lying prostrate beneath the bed. Not a good position to spend a holiday. William was unperturbed and for the rest of the week he serenaded Mia in the middle of the night by howling an overture for his new soul mate for whom he had suffered only unrequited love. This 3am ululation was maddening in the extreme. He was informed that if there was any more of this unseemly behaviour at this time of night his testicles would be history.

The next dog to spend his holiday in the Barn was Merlin, a five-year-old male Golden Retriever who was close to William's size and completely fearless. They became instant pals and tumbled around together taking it in turns to be dominant and subservient as the mood took them. It was good to see them playing on equal terms although at times it rather resembled a 'joust to death' dog fight. Indeed Merlin's owners and I had front row seats but we eventually called 'time' when their teeth clashed as we feared a mouth full of broken teeth and expensive dental treatment. Much later Glennis found that William had sustained a cracked front tooth.

Merlin had spent the first year of his life undergoing intensive training to be a guide dog for the blind until one of his hips was found to have mild dysplasia and he was booted out and sent to a Rescue Centre where he was offered a good home by my holiday makers in exchange for a sizeable donation. They had inherited a one-year-old fully trained dog for a fraction of the £700 going rate and were thrilled with their bargain. Martin's words: "Why not have a fully trained adult dog?" kept haunting me as the voice of reason. Why, I could have been the owner of a willing working dog who would lead me to the shops when my sight or memory failed, or even pop along and fetch The Daily Telegraph (just for the crossword) or drop down to Tesco's and bring home one of everything. In spite of these fanciful flashes I still stubbornly (and crazily) stuck to my desire to train the perfect pet. It was becoming a challenge that my competitive side wanted desperately and perhaps hopelessly to win. Or was I now one of the pack with a wish to dominate and had become the alpha male?

In my garden there was no hint of any problem with Merlin's faulty hips. He could swing them like Elvis into every conceivable position and even many which defied description. He had been castrated but that did nothing to subdue his humping ability which occurred fast and furious like a rhythmic metronome over any part of Wills which surfaced and became unexpectedly available. Wills learned swiftly from the master and added a few sleek moves to his ever growing repertoire, while I learned that castration apparently did little to subdue canine libido.

Meanwhile, up in Scotland Frankie won another first in a Dog Show and was fast becoming quite a threat to other hopeful puppy owners. However, Glennis's delight was short-lived when her beautiful boy let himself down by emptying his bowels in the car coming home. Not the sort of behaviour you expect from an esteemed class champion and red rosette winner.

WILLIAM THE HUNTER

CHRISTINE, one of my PhD students, came to my cottage for a tutorial with Nicola, her Director of Studies. They travelled down from Bristol, a two hour journey, to see my adorable little bundle of fluff. They were met by a caged polar bear performing cartwheels. Christine had kindly brought Wills his first present, a packet of Pedigree Denta Rask deep cleaning bones for healthy teeth and gums. William sat and waited impressively, and on command devoured one of the bones lupine-like in two gulps flat. There was no chewing, no loss of tartar and precious little removal of plaque.

Wills behaved impeccably all day. He was a cool dude basking in the copious attention on offer and enlisted two new members to his fan club. Secretly I knew that the day before he had thrown up and was possibly now feeling one degree under, as he was content to lie under the farmhouse table whilst we were dispensing perceived pearls of wisdom and enjoying a lengthy lunch. He certainly impressed Christine and Nicola who bravely invited him to their homes for the next meetings.

My cunning mutt was able to raise his game many notches and behave impeccably in company, but like children who quickly become bored at home he still played merry hell in the garden. His digging deepened both in the lawn and under the Barn, and he now took delight in rolling in the freshly dug earth. When I called him, I was ignored but when I rattled his liver bones he arrived at my kitchen door with his dreamy chocolate brown eyes looking out from a completely mud caked face and body. My unique pup appeared divinely happy and shamefully guilty in equal measure. He should have been called 'Just William'.

Glennis arrived for a cup of tea with her granddaughter Jordan, who was wearing a long evening glove over one arm, pretending that she had been bitten by her dog, Sky. This four-year-old's imagination ran riot while she recounted the supposed trip to the hospital and the kind nurses who bandaged her arm! Jordan was completely fearless with William. Worryingly so. She had been brought up as one of the pack at her granny's house and thought nothing of rolling around with them. I was very careful to watch Wills who became extremely excited to find a playmate of his own size.

Over tea, Glennis recounted that she had just completed a chapter for a book titled 'Golden Retriever.'. She had been commissioned to write her experience as a breeder on the positives and negatives of finding suitable homes for her puppies. She mentioned that she had based some of her opinion on my experiences. Oh no! I bet William and I erred on to the side of how not to behave! I shuddered. She quickly reassured me that she considered William had a kind and caring home and that single owners often had more time for their pets (phew!).

She also told me that she was about to re-home a pair of three-year-old Retrievers who had never been outside the house, never heard a car, tractor or lorry or even been socialised with other animals. These dogs were nervous wrecks outside their mini environment and needed a home with untold care and kindness, coupled with unlimited understanding. I did not volunteer. I was finding it difficult enough to train a 'normal' puppy, and was clearly not equipped to deal with dogs who were psychologically disturbed. Moreover how would William behave? He was a healthy adolescent male with a one track mind. If I had volunteered to take in these twitchy bitches they would have spent their new found freedom with their backs firmly against the wall.

A group of nurses from the Association for Continence Advice had invited me to lecture at St Pancras Hospital on 'The History of the Male Pelvic Floor' so I left William with Carla and took the train to Paddington at the same time as the exhausted and doleful mob from the Glastonbury music festival were returning home to London to have a bath. On the train there were two types of travellers, those who were wet and caked in mud from head to foot (how do you get your chest muddy?) and those who were desperately trying to avoid touching the ubiquitous unclean.

On the train I read 'Travels with Boogie' by Mark Wallington, a book which recounted the author's journeys, first around the South West peninsular coastline and then later skulling (backwards) up the Thames to its source accompanied by this black 'ugly mutt'. When Boogie's owners divorced, they bickered over who should have the dog. Neither wanted him so he was borrowed by Mark for company on his travels. Boogie was a mongrel's mongrel with no clue to his ancestry and no redeeming features except perhaps his staying power and his love of curry. This book thoroughly amused me especially the extraordinary shapes Mark created when pitching his seven (or was it eight) cornered tent, and like all good books I was sorry when the story ended.

On the return journey more mud-caked passengers joined the train at Castle Carey and travelled South West, occupying every available space. Underneath their mound of equipment they looked like great guys but the rest of us were anxiously trying to avoid being pressed against their muddy anoraks, spattered rucksacks, grubby wet tent and bed rolls.

It was evident when I collected William that he had also been to Glastonbury for he too was in need of a good hose down. He had played with Sky in the garden and kicked up glorious mud prior to wallowing in it hippopotamus-style until his blood was sufficiently cool, and he was caked in the stuff. Mercifully, Carla's fence had been repaired so he was unable to visit the clean and sweet smelling Alsation bitch next door. I took a happy and exhausted reveller home, where, in tune with all lugubrious party animals, he announced he would shower in the morning before crashing out and sleeping round the clock.

In a break in between the showers, one far from balmy evening, I sat on my (damp) garden bench to enjoy the view of Codden Hill in the swirling mist. William was lying down on the lawn watching a tiny baby brown rabbit, who was sitting absolutely still, back straight and ears erect. As Wills seemed unmoved, the young bunny resumed munching the grass rather as if he had happened upon Mr McGregor's vegetable garden. For no apparent reason the little rabbit suddenly sensed danger and bounded under the fence and away into the adjoining field to join the grazing sheep. William sprang into action like a hungry cheetah and chased the bobbing cotton tail as far as the perimeter fence before undertaking a furious burrowing programme, culminating in an even more frenetic sequence of body-flattening in an effort to squeeze under the fence. I tugged him back repeatedly but it was like trying to remove Winnie the Pooh from his honey pot, so I eventually halted procedures by placing a large rock into the deepening burrow. Oh dear, I had placed the anti-rabbit wire netting on the wrong side of the garden.

The very next morning William raced into the garden as if he had an urgent call to nature. However, it was a different and more pressing call to nature that he answered. Two minutes later he arrived triumphantly at my kitchen door with his quarry hanging limply from his mouth. He placed a young brown rabbit at my feet and, before I could save it, he played with it and then rolled on it. I was totally unable to distract William and the poor little rabbit expired. Possibly it was the same brave bunny who had entertained me the previous day. Somehow I could cope with very dead mice but I found it difficult to come to terms with this cruel yet instinctive part of canine behaviour. I wondered who my rabbit killer would attack next. To date, he had killed three mice (four including the one attached to the computer) and one baby rabbit. I shuddered. Was he honing his skills for even larger prey? I preferred not to second guess who was next on the menu.

Meanwhile at yet another dog show, Frankie won another first and proudly accepted his third winner's red rosette. There were no prizes for guessing which puppy was the Champion and which was the Conqueror. I wondered yet again if puppies had been switched prior to collection. In no way did Wills seem to be 'the quiet docile male from the litter'. Perhaps his features were simply inferior to Frankie's for a future in the show ring!

On 07/07/07 at the age of seven months William jumped into the back of the car for the first time. This was not an easy event – for either of us. I lifted up the hatchback and placed some chicken in the car. Nothing happened. William stayed lying down by the kitchen door giving me that all too familiar 'I do not wish to ride in the car' hangdog expression. I lifted him up and half walked him and half dragged him to the boot of the car, all the time moaning out loud about his phenomenal weight. I placed his front paws on the back bumper in preparation for lifting him in when, suddenly and expertly, he jumped in. Even then he ignored the yummy chicken treat as a silent form of protest.

We went to the Green in Landkey hoping for an uneventful walk, so we kept well away from a marquee that was being erected for one of the many weddings taking place on this unique date. William met a little ankle-high wirehaired terrier with no legs, who was aged about a hundred and ten and resembled a boot-cleaning brush. With the passage of time this wily hound had become an exceptionally wise dog. He was amazing; he spotted the enemy, prepared for trouble and froze. William pranced all round him, danced to the front, sniffed at the back and then grew wings and became airborne and flew up and over him in a number of stylish arabesques to try and elicit some sort of a reaction, but he failed miserably to engender even a half-hearted playful response. William eventually gave up the struggle and, to console himself, sped off like a greyhound recently released from his trap to reach his goal, the muddy ditch. I caught him just in time as he was changing colour and led him back, not so gently, to the car. I tried to get him to jump back in, I placed his dirty paws on the bumper but he refused to repeat this feat, leaving me to wonder if it had all been a dream, so I reluctantly lifted my mucky pup back in. On the way home he ignored the piece of roast chicken still lying in the boot in order to give a strong message that he still preferred to take the bus.

Soon he would be taking a boat. Nick and I were trying to find a cottage to rent in Brittany for the winter so that William could use his pristine bright blue passport. The difficulty was finding a property that was close to restaurants that were open in the winter, and more importantly were 'chien' friendly. It seemed as if the French preferred not to have dogs to stay in their villas, even though they are a nation devoted to lap dogs and even allow them to sit on a cushion up to the table in some restaurants. I was disappointed particularly as I let dogs stay in my Barn (with their owners) for summer holiday lets. I tried the British Cottage Owners in France website but it seemed that all their properties were inland and we particularly wanted to walk William along the pink granite coast. I emailed many long term letting agencies and waited for a reply.

Still thinking about France, I made for the supermarket for yet another lorry-load of provisions. Whilst zooming down one of the aisles in an attempt to shop without stopping, I spotted some much cheaper dog food. Tescos had brought out their own brand of Premium Complete Puppy Food in a glossy pack for a bargain price of £2.68p. I compared the ingredients with those contained in IAMS and it seemed as if all the vital vitamins and trace elements were present in the same quantities with the exception of calcium, so provided William had a glass of milk before bedtime we were in line to save a few pounds. This had to be an introductory price and I wondered if I should stock pile and create a puppy food mountain. Even more importantly Wills loved it and hoovered it down without needing a hint of tuna.

William had been on two meals a day since he was six months old. After supper and a play in the garden with his multi-tone and multicoloured squeaky toys he would settle down happily to sleep in his play pen. This confinement was also used for periods of up to four hours whilst I was out working, or for shorter times when I was shopping or playing tennis. My dilemma was: "When could I set him free from his tiger cage?". When I was in the kitchen I could watch him, and if he jumped up to any of the working surfaces I used the reproachful Welsh 'Ah, Ah!' with good effect, but if I was in another room he reverted to nibbling the furniture when he quickly became bored with his toys.

So far, William had barked only for food. He once barked at a pineapple in the fruit bowl but that may have been fear! However, when the very tall (compulsory requirement) meter reader failed to find me home, he reported that my 'ferocious dog' had barked long and loud and nearly jumped out of his cage. So the electric man was responsible for one of those nose marks on the outside of the glass on my kitchen door. I was proud of my new canine home protector, but maybe Wills suspected the visitor was harbouring chicken sandwiches on his person.

The next day I heard a low pitched angry growl interspersed with a programme of fiendish barking, which was enough to alert the hamlet of an imminent nuclear attack. I rushed outside expecting to come face to face with a marauding intruder only to find that William was growling at the dry stone wall. He was barking mad. Worried that he may have found the silver and black adder which was about a yard long, give or take a few stripes, that I saw snaking across my drive last year, I cautiously and bravely investigated and saw a frightened little brown toad squeezed between the stones with no means of escape. I called William inside and kindly invited the amphibian to depart and leave William alone!

I then read in The Daily Telegraph that it was possible to control undue aggression in dogs. Scientists had heralded a new contraceptive pill for male dogs who wished to retain their tackle. Researchers found that a £35 implant containing deslorelin made dogs temporarily infertile and curbed aggressive behaviour by blocking the production of the male hormone testosterone. This effect would last for twelve months and allowed dogs the option of breeding at a later date. However, oral contraceptives for female dogs have been linked to breast cancer and uterine infections so I considered this new pill was not an option for William in view of any possible as yet unknown side-effects. I did not want him to grow man-boobs or develop a squeaky bark, so I opted to ignore this novel medication and instead chose to endure any aggressive barking and discourteous hostility to toads.

Glennis popped in after showing Frankie at yet another Dog Show. True to form, he had won another first picking up his fifth winner's rosette (he had demurely kept one of his triumphs quiet). My friend has shown dogs for many years but has never had a dog who has been such a consistent star. As an international judge, Glennis knew what puppy features were necessary to produce a champion class Retriever and she chose Frankie for his strong head, thick fur and imposing posture.

My cousin Claire, husband Karl and daughter Julia came to visit and to spend a week in the Barn. We took William down the lane so that we could play Pooh sticks in the river, and then ventured along the otter-free Tarka trail. This walk commenced with my highly expensively trained puppy lying prone on the grass bank next to my cottage and despite multiple cajoling refused to budge. This was his easy way of gaining attention and looking cute. We walked ahead and he swiftly changed his mind and enjoyed running free under the stile and beside the river with Julia, and before long both players were splashing each other happily in the fast flowing water. This was enormously entertaining and a wonderful way of spending time together but the Pooh sticks game ended in stalemate for all contestants as a fallen tree had become firmly wedged under the bridge and prevented any of our sticks from floating downstream, constituting another important job for The River Clearance Authority!

Cousin Claire, Julia and I visited Bucks Mills, a delightful beach reached by a steep footpath descending from the pretty village. William adored Julia and followed her across the beach like a shadow, bounding over the rocks and pebbles and narrowly skirting a waterfall that crashed noisily onto the stones below. Julia, aged almost fourteen, decided to scale the cliff and confidently ascended like a skilled mountaineer leaving William at the bottom to watch and admire. Two minutes later he jumped halfway up the sheer rock face to join her. This was the same dog who refused to jump into the back of the car! We held our breath expecting either a nasty accident or, at the very least, the need for an emergency message to the coastguard requesting urgent rescue of 'Puppy stuck on cliff ledge!' but incredibly, as Julia climbed slowly down, William descended like a nimble mountain goat while the crowd who had amassed beneath to watch the potential disaster breathed a collective sigh of relief. After that shock, Julia stayed at sea level and explored the surrounding rock pools looking for shrimps whilst Claire threw seaweed at the water's edge for a particularly electrically charged William, the only dog on the beach turning cartwheels.

My son, Martin told us of a far scarier incident that he had experienced whilst walking along the cliff path from Coombe Martin to Hunter's Inn with his Jack Russell. During the walk Paddy suddenly leapt into the air and with one swift move caught a pheasant. Martin decided that it was unwise to be seen carrying a game bird so he flung it over the cliff. At the same instant Paddy sprang skywards to retrieve his prize, only to be stopped from jumping clear over the cliff edge by his quick-thinking owner. Martin still trembles when he thinks of what could have happened.

William and Julia bonded together like frisky and impulsive teenagers enjoying the new found freedom coupled with curiosity that accompanies youth. When Julia left, these faithful holiday companions missed each other and the many and diverse dollops of fun they shared together. Julia returned home to prepare for choir school, and William was due to spend another term at boarding school while Nick whisked me away to undertake some fjord spotting in Norway, safe in the knowledge that William would be happily looked after in Wales.

This time I wanted William's training to concentrate on walking to heel when he was impatient to reach his favourite destinations, be they parks, rivers or the sea. For example, at Bucks Mills he sniffed the ozone and launched himself downhill at the speed of light while I tried desperately to control him. He was a strong lad who directed all his food, energy and exercise to muscle hypertrophy and probably secretly attended a Charles Atlas body-building programme.

I packed for Norway with consummate care, making sure I included clothes for every type of weather, then popped a pile of food in a box for William and left home in the pouring rain, only to find when I reached Merthyr Tidfil that I was still wearing my slippers! I held an umbrella in one hand and led my treasured pet down a wet slope to his boot camp. William bounded in with such force that for the first time I had to let go of the lead otherwise I would have become yet another granny casualty statistic. He was eager to see Gwyneth and all the staff at his second and obviously preferred home, the chipolata emporium.

Nick and I thoroughly enjoyed seeing the spectacularly

stunning Nordic scenery by car en route from Trondheim to Bodo with a variety of sightseeing detours. We spent many hours looking in a number of regions for the elusive moose resulting in a sighting of exactly none (except in the zoo, and one stuffed in the Arctic Centre) but we were successful in seeing six sea eagles and a pair of cranes. Every time I saw someone with a Retriever I missed young Wills even though I was reassured that he was also having a ball in Wales. Interestingly I saw only champagne-coloured Retrievers which possibly were chosen to blend in with their owners' wonderful Scandinavian blonde hair, another instance of the dog selected to mirror its owner.

After our amazing holiday I went to collect William and was directed to a field where he displayed total obedience whilst walking smartly to heel with Gwyneth and her stock of sausages. He also lay down to command and stayed down. In this environment he performed faultlessly for me. Daniel, one of the trainers who bred Retrievers, commented that William was a great dog and that the bump on his head would divide when his face filled out. Presumably he would then sport two bumps! Daniel also announced that I must be ready for my next Retriever now. Wrong! One best friend was quite enough. Two puppies needed two owners not one. Puppies were like grandchildren who should never under any circumstances outnumber their adult carers. I was advised to purchase a half choke chain as he had outgrown his existing puppy collar and was shown that this type of collar was kind to the dog but gave a noise when it was tweaked. I was advised to pull the lead firmly if he laid down defiantly, which was behaviour he saved especially and only for me as I led him to the car!

CHAPTER 10

BAD MANNERS

ON ARRIVING HOME from Norway with my freshly
trained hero, I learned that Frankie had collected
another First Prize. He now had won two firsts at
Open Shows and five firsts at Championship Shows. One first
at a Championship Show was sufficient to qualify for entry to
Crufts so Frankie had quintuple qualification and was well
on his way to Retriever stardom and a rampant career as a
much desired stud.

William on the other hand was to stay as a loveable and
loving pet. I telephoned Jeanine, one of the physiotherapists
with whom I had trained many eons ago at The Royal
London, Hospital, before it had gained its royal status, to see
if she would like me to visit her. It was a kind of cheering up
mission. Jeanine had recently undergone carotid artery
surgery, having experienced a series of mini strokes, and was
still rather weak and wobbly. She insisted that I brought
William to be company for their elderly dog, Clyde, as his
sister, Bonnie, had recently died and he was in need of some
company. I think that when people think of puppies they
conjure up images of cute, comforting cuddliness. I took great
pains to explain that William, who was now eight months old,
was the size of a horse, became wildly excitable with every
new experience and would jump up uncontrollably until he
was exhausted. Jeanine suggested that we should take the
dogs for a walk and I unwisely relented.

I arrived at Jeanine and Peter's beautiful converted stables
in Ottery St Mary at the same time as Michael, one of Jeanine's
bridge playing friends, who was also visiting his convalescing
friend. He limped in using crutches having just had the

plaster removed from his leg following a fracture of his fibula, which he had sustained slipping on wet grass down a rock face. I kept William on his lead. Clyde barked whilst William growled so Peter and I decided that Wills would feel less threatened off his lead. This was a poor and crass decision on my part. William made a dash for Clyde who ran off while William gave chase by bounding through the space between Michael's injured foot and his crutch. Fortunately Jeanine's physiotherapy skills saved Michael from falling and we helped him to a chair whilst I apologised profusely and then offered further heartfelt regrets.

In the next few moments we quickly realized that these dogs had no interest in each other whatsoever. William was more interested in flattening the lavender, but after much cajoling preferred to sit meekly in Bonnie's favourite spot under the shade of an acacia tree, and we were able to enjoy tea and home-made chocolate cake on the terrace in the glorious summer sunshine. I gave William a much needed bowl of water while Clyde reached up to drink from an ancient horse trough. Then the unthinkable happened! William spied the water and jumped in. In the blink of an eyelid the peace and tranquillity of that happy tea party were shattered for ever. Peter and Jeanine both exhibited acute apoplexy and shouted in unison: "It's seven feet deep!", whereupon Peter grabbed hold of the shocked, flailing and extremely sodden dog and heaved him out of the trough. Why did horses need a trough so deep? Did they practise equine hydrotherapy in those days? My questions went unasked and unanswered. This was the time to make our departure. I wisely decided against walking William in company, said that I was delighted to find Jeanine looking so well (despite the apoplexy), made a swift exit and took my wet, evil-smelling water-lover home before he caused any further damage.

Dear diary, please remind me not to bring William with me to Jeanine's home again until he is ancient and doddering.

William was far from being anything of the kind. The next day I spent gardening, mainly uprooting dead poppies, removing stinging nettles and severing stray brambles that threatened to invade my garden like prickly persistent trifids. William was a star. He was great company and enjoyed himself watching me work and accompanying my many journeys to the compost heap with an over-heaped wheelbarrow. I could not believe that this was the same animal who had played merry hell at Jeanine's. I would like to say we were a team. Perhaps we were. He was the overseer and I the worker, a pecking order that seemed to suit us both just fine. This was altogether a better scenario than when he was single-mindedly uprooting my plants and I was the helpless and distraught onlooker.

Sadly he still had his junior moments. I had a grandfather, father and son of six holidaying in the Barn. I was most concerned about William being alone with the little boy and voiced my thoughts to his granddad, who said I was not to worry as they had a dog at home and they understood dogs. I continued my cautions until the grandfather stopped me in my tracks by saying: "All right, we have been warned!". However, later in the week they hung washing on the gate to dry. To William this must have been heaven sent and he allowed himself a puppy moment of exquisite purity: he attacked a designer tee shirt and reduced it to a riot of ragged ribbons. I was left puzzled as to who was to blame. William was a puppy with normal puppy tendencies and therefore not culpable. I was totally oblivious to this event until much later, though I did consider it was possibly unwise to leave clothes, or anything for that matter, in a garden that was patrolled by an attack hound. I altered my 'Barn Welcome' information to include a warning about the hazards of leaving clothes or equipment in the garden in reach of the puppy. It read just short of saying there was a monster clothes' shredder on the prowl.

I was scheduled to attend the International Continence Society Annual Meeting in Rotterdam for six days, where among other duties I had accepted the honour of chairing the physiotherapy session in the main auditorium. I had agreed to this in haste when I felt rather important but now regretted my decision as the magnitude of this burden set in. In fact I felt intimidated at the very thought of it and would rather have prepared a lecture and delivered it than have to speak off the cuff to such a vast and esteemed international audience. I left William with Carla and flew off.

On my return I telephoned Carla to see if it was convenient to collect William and to hear how he had behaved. She replied: "I'll tell you when I see you". Oh dear, ominous words. I knew William was capable of an ever increasing range of misdemeanours and my imagination ran riot. When I drove up William was sitting on the pavement. Apparently he had bitten through both ends of a plastic waste pipe, had repeatedly mounted Carla's dog, Sky, and had climaxed in chewing through a door post. When I asked to see the door post, I was refused permission leaving me with the unhappy thought that perhaps there was no door post left to see! To add insult to his list of sins he had howled at five o'clock in the morning and elicited verbal complaints from the unhappy and now less friendly neighbours. At home William barked only for food. He was used to grazing as there was no competition with another dog. Maybe Sky had snacked sneakily on his dinner?

The next day was a glorious sunny day with a perfect blue sky kissing the spectacular panorama of rolling hills beyond reminding me why I had chosen this joyous part of Devon, and as I walked round and admired my garden a very much thinner William refused to leave my side. He had wolfed his breakfast greedily and then barked for more. The lad was hungry. I decided to ask the Vet if they could recommend suitable kennels for the future for my snaked hipped hound regretting that Merthyr Tidfil and Gwyneth were so far away. Out in the garden William walked behind a seat set in a stone wall and started barking. He stared at something, looked startled and then barked while bouncing backwards in one startled movement before repeating this strange behaviour again and again. I investigated cautiously in case he had found a deadly adder or even a dog-eating toad and discovered that he was barking at my green wheelbarrow. The gardener had left it lying on its side, whereas I had always left it upstanding so that it filled up with rainwater in which William was prone to splash and assuage his thirst. As soon as I had righted the barrow he stopped looking anxious, became quiet and appeased and slunk away obviously frightfully grateful to receive a little help from his friend. He repaid this kindness by indulging himself with my blackberries.

I decided to find a caring kennels for William when I was away lecturing. I had kept the first six months of his life relatively free so that I could be with him while he was growing up and now I found I was fully booked for September, October and early November. I did not want him to finish eating Carla's doorpost if there was anything left to eat so I scoured the inserts in the Yellow Pages for local boarding kennels. I telephoned the first one that I found and was told "We only take cats." which was a bitter blow as they were the nearest and therefore quite handy. I decided against painting my pet with tiger stripes and continued the hunt. The phone at Springfield Kennels, Lovacott Green Cottage at Newton Tracey was engaged, so I popped in the car to see where they were situated and stopped to ask for directions at Lovacott Green Farm. It was a surprise to find that my tennis playing friend, Muriel, lived next door to the kennels and she warmly recommended her neighbours Linda and John Chalk.

Linda told me that William would have to undergo a trial period of one day to see if he could cope with kennel life and (I guess more importantly), if they could cope with him. Nick gave this trial a fifty fifty chance of success. I was considerably more optimistic. I neatened him up and took my willing lamb for his kennel test. Like the professional he was, he excelled. John gave him a nine out of ten report before telling me that he never ever gave any dog the ultimate accolade of ten out of ten. What a hero (John as well). I duly booked him in for a few days while I was away lecturing, but just when I was feeling much happier about Will's holiday arrangements Linda told me that they always closed down in November!

I came home to prepare for my dinner guests. I had invited Jennie and Sally, my two sex therapist friends, to a vegetarian dinner. I sent them an email:

Dear Esteemed Dinner Guests

Please could you dress accordingly:

No silk dangly bits
No chiffon
No flowing ribbons

No swishy skirts
And not too many sequins

With lots of love
William

PS I am not very obedient despite having been to an extremely
expensive boarding school and I get very excited when I see
beautiful people.

Sally emailed back immediately saying that now she had
nothing to wear. Jennie failed to receive her email and arrived
in a pretty swishy skirt.

In honour of my guests I began a belated and much needed,
and a tad delayed, Spring cleaning programme. It was more
a kind of woodlouse and cobweb removal exercise. Like all
serious housework, it commenced by emptying out the
plastic dust box from the vacuum cleaner. I took the filter
outside, held my breath and banged it against the gate elicit-
ing a cloud of lethal grey brown dust while trying desperately
not to inhale. Suddenly through the murky mist I spied
William smiling like a supercilious Cheshire cat and proudly
holding the dust box lid in his mouth. When I asked him to
'Fetch' he bounced away backwards with a defiant "Catch me
if you can!" expression. I pursued him with a box of his
favourite gravy bone biscuits without a wisp of success, and
it was only when I emptied the complete box of biscuits onto
the lawn that he deigned to drop the now badly chewed lid.
I still had a lot to learn about puppies and their ability to
benefit from a momentary lack of thought. I guess anything
on the floor was a toy in William's eyes. I had to improve but
sadly, this improvement phase was woefully short. It ended
abruptly when I noticed, out of the corner of my eye, a disin-
genuous William disappearing down the garden triumphantly clenching my precious feather duster in his teeth!

I feared that William had too few toys. I was sitting down
enjoying my dinner whilst doing the crossword one evening
when I noticed William lying on his back admiring two
glands that had appeared either side of his penis, which were
quite distinct from his large, plum like and similarly coloured

testicles. Without so much as a 'by your leave' he bent forwards and open mouthed, teeth flashing, attacked his tackle with the sensitivity of a rutting boar. Indeed, he completely swallowed his pride. It was all over in two minutes flat leaving William exhausted and, I guess, happy. My questions were: 'Shouldn't we have had dinner first?' and 'How often was this likely to happen?'.

How sad that William was doomed to a life of self-stimulation when his father, Reggie was enjoying the pleasures of a working as a stud on a regular basis thanks to the fame and acclaim of his champion son, Frankie, who was destined for a similar career. I looked into the future. Frankie would thrill while Willy wanked.

I decided to improve my act when I passed my local pet shop and saw a photograph of a Golden Retriever walking happily into the car using a ramp. I was still having problems lifting my wayward hound into the car so I spent £89, give or take a few pence, to purchase this helpful equipment. At the ripe old age of nine months, William was about to ascend into the boot of the car in style using his own runway, a form of conveyance usually reserved for dogs of advancing years. As the ramp was so heavy and the pet shop was in the pedestrian precinct, I organised to have it delivered, and indeed it arrived home before I did. It was not a smart move. It weighed in at 13.5kilograms which was more than the whacking weight of Wills. I should have sussed what a heavy and awkward contraption it would be when I was in the shop. I had to lift it out of the back of the car, open out the three hinged parts and turn it over for my dog to walk up. I called William. He was not co-operative. I led him gently up the slope but he kept bounding off perversely first to one side then the other like the mischievous and comical dogs in 'The Underdog' TV programme, so I forced him up by a system of collar tugging and butt pushing until my unhappy brute was cowering in the boot. What a palaver!

Having captured my pet, I drove to the Millennium Green for our usual outing and I spoke to a few dog owners about the trials and tribulations of puppy ownership. "Your dog is a puppy!" they remarked in disbelief. "I've never seen a puppy that size!". When I returned to the car with my outsized monster I was unable to hold him while I assembled the ramp so I popped his front paws on the boot sill and heaved him into the car in the usual tried and tested fashion, wondering if the pet shop would reimburse me for one slightly used ramp. What a disappointment!

The next day I rose early, as elderly people do, to drive to the pet shop before ten o'clock when the area became a pulsating pedestrian haven. When I mentioned the impossible weight of the ramp, I was shown a much lighter model from the back of the shop costing £75 and weighing only 7.5kilograms. Why was I not shown this before? I became dubious as it still meant I had to assemble the walkway while holding a reluctant, recalcitrant dog so I gratefully received a refund and promised to think about it.

Nick telephoned from Ireland with news of a high density polyethylene sliding ramp on the internet which could be kept in the boot. I opened the www.overthetop.co.uk website and found the contraption. It weighed 18lbs (8.16 kilograms) and cost £99.99 + £7.99 carriage (it was called 'Over the top' after all!) but it needed four feet of boot length, which was ideal for Nick's Range Rover but too long for my diddy VW Golf. Nick considered purchasing one in preparation for our holiday in France in November when we were bravely taking Wills abroad as he realised that it would be his duty to pipe my gigantic puppy aboard. Personally I think he should have purchased a harness and hoist, or a rear-loading lift, or maybe even a catapult, but if this ramp failed its purpose I could always use it to get into the passenger seat, which was very much higher than normal cars and had always given me a problem unless we were parked close to the kerb or Nick remembered to press the car-lowering mechanism. It was not a good time to raise the topic that William happily hopped aboard buses like a bunny because we were not about to tour France by omnibus. Sensibly, Nick had purchased a set of washable boot lining covers similar to those that he had kindly given me for my car, and which had proved to be such a boon.

It was when my special school friend Jenny came to stay for the weekend that William decided to impress. He brought a freshly killed baby thrush to the steps leading to my kitchen door and batted it about in a vain attempt to rekindle its air-borne attributes. This awful assault added to his dearly departed death list of four mice (including the computer mouse), one baby rabbit and now one innocent young bird. That night at 2.30am he was sick as a parrot in his play pen so I let him outside whilst I cleared up. I waited and waited for him to return, finished the crossword, and still he refused to come back inside so I investigated, Sherlock Holmes style, with a high beamed torch searching every corner of my garden, wearing only my flowing dressing gown and bedroom slippers. My Dear Watson would have been proud of me. I found him (William not Watson) in a corner of the lawn rolling in the wet grass, slathering at the mouth and holding his tummy in the manner of a polar bear with parox-ysms of peristaltic pain. I enticed him back to the kitchen to brush him down and comfort my aching friend. Eventually I was able to return to bed at 3.30am. In the morning, while I was suffering the side effects of a broken night's sleep, William was back to his normal energetic self and ate a hearty breakfast in preparation for another day's avid stalking. I dearly wished I was capable of revoking his predator's licence to kill.

I particularly needed some beauty sleep, even some unin-terrupted sleep without a hint of beauty would have done, as the previous night I had also been up from 2.30am to 3.30am due to a freak accident. In my slumbers I had somehow knocked the large brass bedside light onto my head. I woke up with an acutely sore head clutching the lamp and with blood streaming out through my nose. Knowing that this was a serious symptom of a head injury I immediately and sensi-bly dialled 999. 'What was my telephone number, address and name? How did the accident happen? Was I alone in the house?' they asked, and 'Could I get dressed and open the door?'. In my shocked and trembling state I had completely forgotten that my daughter, Claire and friend, Jenny were staying with me!

Within five minutes William announced the arrival of the paramedics, Sara and Anne. "Please could you remove the dog?" they asked. William was in his cage totally intrigued with my new colouring and was going nowhere. My hair had become bright red on one side and my face was totally, yes totally, covered in rivers of blood like a gory photograph from the war zone. Apparently head injuries are renowned for their profuse bleeding. Sara gently washed my face and hair and found a laceration about a centimetre long and a large haematoma (egg) on the parietal region of my head which fortunately had started to congeal. I was therefore spared any head shaving or stitches or, more importantly, a lengthy visit to the hospital by these professional paramedics. They were wonderfully calming as they checked my pulse, blood pressure, eyesight and made sure I was compos mentis and not any dizzier than usual. Jenny kindly made us all a hot drink and changed the blood stained bed linen that would have made Dracula proud.

I was intrigued as to how this accident could have happened. My daughter Claire's imagination ran wild as she stuck to her flights of fantasy that her mother was drunk, which was far from the truth, but made a good story (for her). "Mother hit her head in a drunken stupor!" I could hear her telling her many friends. The next morning I telephoned Nick to ask if I flailed my arms around in my sleep. "How would I know?", he swiftly replied. "I always sleep with a pillow over my head!" Then he announced that he was going to find me a rubber bedside lamp similar to the old fashioned rubber chamber pots available only to lunatics!

I felt this was a little unfair until the next day when I turned up at North Devon District Hospital to find the Ladywell Unit firmly closed. After I had knocked on every office door and found no secretary at home, I not so speedily surmised that they were all at an important meeting. I was miffed at not being invited. It was only after noticing that the car park was indeed empty that it dawned on me that it was Sunday and not Monday. Was I this dizzy professor before or after the bump on the head?

Once I had returned to my senses, I decided to move both my heavy Laura Ashley lamps to the far side of the bedside tables, making it almost impossible to reach the switches, but as far away from my sleepy head as possible. For good measure, and to keep Social Services at bay, I took down the beautiful Alphonse Mucha pictures that hung over the bed head lest they mysteriously go 'bump in the night' and crack my head open again. I then needed something light to hang on the exposed picture hooks that weighed less than a hovering dragon fly, so I went shopping.

Shopping produced not a whisper of success. Nick thought it a touch extreme to take down the pictures over the bed so he sent me a card of a cute blonde Retriever puppy wearing a pale blue knitted bobble hat. Inside he wrote 'Perhaps you should wear a hat in bed!'.

If I needed a hat, William needed a muzzle. He had, to date, chewed his squeaky green crocodile to pieces, decimated his purple plastic hedgehog and played havoc with the duck that Nick had kindly given me when I was recovering from surgery some years before. This duck was the large fluffy job, not the vibrating duck for use in the bath! I then recalled that Wills had found this yellow creature in the children's toy basket and had left piles of golden fluff all over the lawn the day before he threw up. Oops, another mistake, I had blamed the wrong bird!

CHAPTER 11

THE WOUNDED SOLDIER

I LEFT MY four-legged muncher at Springfield Boarding Kennels while I went to Estoril to lecture to fifty physio-therapists who had arrived from all corners of Portugal and who mercifully spoke English. William had attained nine out of ten for his kennel trial so I was concerned that he may not be able to keep up this previous giddy level of achieve-ment. I had to leave him for a few days as I had to fly direct from London Airport. The return journey to Devon was one of the worst that I had ever taken. The M4 was thick with a gloomy grey spray that blotted out the silhouettes of all the vehicles and completely occluded their brake lights. In those ghastly conditions it was no surprise that there had been an accident, which meant all the traffic travelled at less than walking pace for more than three junctions. After four hours I stopped sensibly at a hotel in Bristol at close to midnight, knowing that I had no hope of reaching Devon that day.

When I collected William he had been given a metaphorical gold star. John was extremely effusive about his lack of chewing, his obedience when waiting to be fed and his will-ingness to come when called. (Had Wills upped his game or had he been mistaken for another dog?). This was not the pet I knew! He had come to his name without a whistle or a lengthy rattle of the liver bone box! It was rather like receiv-ing a glowing school report for my children and I basked in the reflected and non-reflected glory. Wills had been exercis-ing with Jip, a red Setter, who had outpaced him across the field but was then totally unable to match his stamina, so crashed out with exhaustion leaving the playful puppy wanting more and more fun. And to cap it all John was so complimentary about William's look and physique when compared with all the other Retrievers he had known that he wanted a portrait taken. Perhaps William could become a top model and charge per pose to offset his costly kennel fees?

Sadly, I had to leave William yet again. This time I chose another kennel to prevent the RSPCA from deeming me neglectful, so I took my best friend, who was now ten months old, to Towsers Country Kennels where Sue and Shaun promised to look after him as their own. I flew up to Aberdeen and back in a day for a meeting at the University and rushed to collect Wills the next day. The report I received was good; he had been obedient and behaved impeccably. Shaun noticed he was quick to learn even though he flatly refused to sit and wait politely before meals. William was learning defiance! I opened the gate to my waiting car and the heavy cast iron catch dropped on to my thumb and sent it throbbing all the way home, while I cursed quietly to myself and promised to take more care of my digits.

William arrived home to find Goochi, a smartly clipped Airedale belonging to the Barn guests, in the garden. Unexpectedly, within minutes they fought over a ball which culminated in a bitten paw for poor Wills. I should have been wary of Airedales ever since the chimney restorer was attacked. I removed my dog from the garden lest he developed aggressive tendencies unknown to his breed and took him indoors where he pointedly licked and nursed his puncture wound.

The next day (my birthday) I woke up late totally surprised that William had not barked as usual at 7.30am. He was quietly lying in his bed with a sad, soulful expression. I noticed his paw had become swollen and was now twice its normal size. I rang the veterinary surgery for an immediate appointment and saw a vet named Simon who popped my puppy onto the scales where he weighed a staggering 32.5Kg. He was concerned that the infection had entered William's joint or tracked up the tendon sheath so he was given a shot of antibiotic and some large palatable (I hoped) antibiotic and anti-inflammatory pills to consume. Simon deftly applied a poultice and the nurse fashioned him a ridiculously large and cumbersome lampshade. William felt silly and point blank refused to budge. A young spaniel entered the clinic but William was much too embarrassed to show a smidgeon of interest. He was rooted to the spot. It was only after I had removed the lampshade that he deigned to limp to the car. Poor William was suffering such obvious pain coupled with a large helping of abject indignity. When we arrived home I replaced the lampshade, whereupon Wills sat with his back to me in the mother of all sulks and then spent the rest of the day reclining with a hangdog expression designed to melt the most hardened human and, on a day which should have been happy, reduced me to tears. The only silver lining to the cloudy day came from the thought that Marks and Spencer would pick up the £103.67 bill and I smugly congratulated myself for choosing an insurance policy without an excess. That night William refused to lie down and spent the night standing up whimpering mournfully.

This nocturnal sighing pulled at the very fibre of my heart and into the pit of my stomach and continued until I lay William down and then applied the collar, but it was less intrusive than the noise in the middle of the night heard by a Scottish Lady who awoke to the most unholy banging, clanging and clattering in her castle. When she bravely investigated she found that the horns of the premature lamb she was raising had become completely stuck in a metal waste paper basket into which a guest had thrown an apple core. She managed to free the lamb without resorting to the fire brigade, unlike the dear little boy who made headlines recently when his head became firmly stuck in a traffic cone! The next day my helmet-wearing wounded soldier wandered into the garden for his early morning pee when he suddenly caught sight of a rabbit. He thundered across the lawn to scoop it up in his new shovel. Only a blind rabbit would have failed to notice this freak of nature advancing towards him in full battle gear. The bunny neatly hopped into the blackberries like a snooker ball disappearing into a pocket while William limped slowly back to me looking like a cat who was completely out of cream.

The new Barn guests arrived with a delightful Cocker Spaniel puppy aged just 15 weeks. Within minutes William returned to his normal active self. He was very gentle with the puppy but in the adrenaline rush completely forgot about his bandaged appendage. Rather like a child who bounces back in the blink of an eye to renewed and revitalized health, Wills was rapidly on the road to recovery.

I had to leave William with Linda and John at Springfield Kennels while I was lecturing at the Annual Conference of Irish Continence Nurses and Physiotherapists in Portlaoise. I telephoned the day before to see if they would care for a dog who was on drugs. They were more than happy to oblige, so that morning I removed the poultice and with it a bucket-full of purulent gunge and packed William's bag to include his wounded paw medication. I also took his far-from-favourite lampshade to the kennels and flew to the fair city.

On my return I rushed straight from Exeter Airport to collect my hoodie. When he was feeding and exercising he had this contraption removed and became his normal happy self, but when he was dressed to kill, he sat pointedly with his back to the door displaying in no uncertain terms a fit of the grumps.

Thereafter the circumposed collar was removed for feeding and for all trips into the garden and walks down the lane, but it was replaced when Wills was indoors and in scab attack mode. It seemed as if William had developed a split person-ality which ranged from manic depressive sulking when framed in angelic white plastic to pure manic elation when the hideous shade was removed. Would Wills be left with a lasting psychosis? Would he need a shrink?

I think it was me who was in need of a shrink! I returned William to Springfield kennels before traveling to Bucking-hamshire for a reunion with my fellow physiotherapy stu-dents. It was only when I reached the kennels (twenty minutes away in the opposite direction) that I remembered I had left the remaining antibiotics on the kitchen table! I returned home to collect Wills's pills whilst I (very quietly) cursed my failing memory.

Our physiotherapy set met for lunch at the Nag's Head in Great Missenden and this year, for the first time, husbands were invited provided they could cope with our girlish giggles. It was an amazing 43 years since we qualified as basic grade physiotherapists and were flung out as raw recruits to earn our living on a meager salary of £10 per week. As the years turned, the topic of conversation at our reunions changed from careers, to babies, to children, to hysterectomies, to children's weddings, to grandchildren, to retirement and now, would you believe it, to dogs.

Jeanine and Peter lost no time in recounting the outrageous but sadly true tale of the exuberant and totally untrained William's first (and last) visit to Ottery St Mary. Apparently my good friends had dined out ever since on our day of total disaster making William infamous throughout the bridge playing community of Devon and surrounding card shuffling counties. I collapsed like a pack of cards as I anticipated the story about to unfold. They related the epic day without knobs and whistles as there was no need for a hint of exaggeration or a whisper of embellishment. My best friend was likened to 'Just William' while everyone was amazed at the horrendous havoc that one expensively-trained pedigree pup could produce in under one hour.

Jeanine and Peter could see the humorous side as they gaily recalled William nearly flooring their crutch dependent friend, then depositing an enormous turd (Peter's words not mine) in the middle of the lawn, followed by flattening the lavender, nearly drowning in their pool and then, for the unforgettable finale, winding his extendable lead completely around a trembling Jeanine, whom we had come to cheer up. While they were giggling, my sense of the ridiculous was completely crushed as I flushed, nay blushed, under the heavy burden of puppy responsibility. Then to prove the point, Jeanine happily announced that their late, much loved, Bonnie would now be replaced by a mature, fully trained and totally obedient dog from the canine rescue centre. William had put my dear friends off puppies for life!

My beloved fluffy puppy became a fearsome ram now he had mastered his new weapon. He swiftly learned that he could butt my shins (and my butt!) using his collar as horns as he ran ram-shod into my now bruised and battered legs. When I removed the offending shade he deftly devoured the black scab from his paw which only extended the time he needed to wear his attack helmet. Once kitted out, he projected his barking by gruffly using this amplifier in a similar way to the antique gramophones of my youth depicting 'His Master's Voice'. The sad, woeful, lugubrious look swiftly disappeared and was replaced by the roaring rage of a thunderous and wilful warrior ready for his very own Armageddon.

The warrior retreated into his shell like a giant tortoise with agoraphobia when the next Barn Guests arrived. They were accompanied, would you believe, by another upstanding Airedale. William's wound had healed and his collar removed but his nerves were still in tatters. He shunned the new arrival and, instead of playing puppy-like with this eager dog, he ran indoors to the security and safety of his cage. It seemed as if one Airedale had ruined it for all the other terriers in the pack, just as one crusty crocodile could ruin it for all the others sporting a similarly menacing jaw-line.

My warrior defended me that night when I was woken by bellicose barking followed by a tap on the glass window of my kitchen door. I went downstairs to find a fireman standing outside trying to make himself heard. I reckoned he was not there to steal, plunder or rape, dressed in such bulky protective gear surmounted by the hugest helmet that it was possible to wear without his knees buckling, so I invited him inside. Once inside my man in uniform removed his helmet and with it (apparently) his hair. His bald head was reduced to the size and shape of an overly generous goose egg. William went ballistic. He barked louder than a bull elephant with toothache and with every bark he jumped higher than before in an attempt to clear his cage and orbit the moon.

Apparently the caravan in the field at the top of the hill was ablaze and the firemen wanted to trace the owners. I said that I hoped desperately that they were not inside. I sent him to the neighbouring farm and congratulated William for being so brave (or frightened) before settling my dreadfully disturbed dog down for the night.

Evidently William was taking his guard dog duties seriously. This episode made me realize that no-one, in whatever dishabille, dress or disguise, could enter my house without Wills announcing their arrival. The nagging thought that someone had hit me over the head with my bedside lamp, like the crusty keeper of the candlestick in Cluedo, was forever laid to rest.

I had to lecture to physiotherapists and nurses in Ireland, so I led William to the car in preparation for a visit to the Towsers holiday camp as a welcome change from walking up and down the lane to order on a limp lead. To my surprise he jumped in with the sangfroid of a graceful grasshopper. I cuddled my clever chum and offered copious congratulations to bolster his ever increasing confidence but hoped his newly found hubris would not invite a return to his former ways.

I arrived back too late to collect William as I had been delayed for two and a half hours at Dublin Airport, reportedly because of a minor aircraft fault, but more likely to have been due to a serious tip off, because our boarding passes were checked (again) and we were sniffed by a bonnie black Labrador dog to see if we smelt both explosive and drug-free. I telephoned Sue from Towsers and she agreed that I could collect William that evening. He had experienced some galloping diarrhoea and was feeling many degrees below par. My guilt at leaving him increased exponentially. Naturally he declined to leap into the car and lay low for two days before he resumed his normal high spirited antics in time for a visit from my gorgeous granddaughters, Maggie and Charlie, when he almost flipped out of his pen like a halibut intent on turning handsprings.

CHAPTER 12

WILLIAM GOES ON HOLIDAY

IN PREPARATION for our holiday to Brittany, Nick lined the back of his Range Rover with specially designed protective material, assembled a dog cage and placed it inside. Fortunately it fitted. We packed the car with enough toys, treats and dog food for three weeks and set off for Plymouth where we stopped on the Hoe to give Wills his last walk before boarding the 10pm ferry. At security William's new blue pet passport was checked and we were given a portable scanner to identify the serial number on his microchip. Then we were given a large shocking-pink sticker bearing a black paw mark to place on the windscreen with the words 'PET ON BOARD' clearly marked.

The crossing was extremely rough and turbulent and from the luxury of our cabin I was concerned about poor William who had to spend the night alone in the car. I need not have worried for in the morning he was clean, dry and happy but even happier when we found an empty lorry park close to the dock in Roscoff for him to balance on three legs for a 'longer than ever before' morning pee.

We arrived half an hour later in the beautiful town of Morlaix where we were warmly welcomed by Stafford and Jenny Taylor from 'Le Manoir de Coat Amour' who owned the gîte where we would be staying for three weeks. They were looking after a gentle Golden Retriever named Phoebe for the 'Le Chien et l'Enfant' organisation which placed placid dogs with children who had experienced bereavement and those who sadly had physical or mental disabilities. This wonderful idea reminded me of a programme I had seen on television where an autistic boy had started to emerge from his inner world once he had been given a dog of his own to care for and subsequently love. All Phoebe's food and vet bills were paid by the organisation and in return she was expected to produce a litter of puppies. After the last 'mating' by artificial insemination, depriving Phoebe of her little bit of fun, she registered her distaste with a false pregnancy and ballooned in size due not only to her voracious appetite but to the fact that Stafford thought that she was eating for an expectant litter. Phoebe instantly befriended William, and all his manly bits so he extended this friendship by inviting her to his first birthday party on December 5th.

On arrival our first consideration was to book an appointment with the vet for the day before our departure. Jenny kindly gave us the name of a local 'Docteur Vétérinaire' who not only made our appointment but sold us some holiday anti-tick and flea lotion to prevent Continental dog-eating parasites.

For the first two days William stayed tentatively by our sides while we explored the 12 acre garden and the convenient footpath running alongside, which replaced an old railway line and seemed to stretch for miles. Suddenly he saw an elderly French lady on the footpath and surprised her by jumping up, leaving muddy footprints on her white raincoat. We apologised for our overgrown puppy in our best French and from then on kept William on the lead unless the footpath was deserted – or at least seemed to be. One day a young French guy appeared from nowhere and ran past us with two Retrievers. William joined the pack and they all ran into the distance round a bend and out of sight. This speeding Pied Piper failed to stop! I was scared we would never see William again and imagined this lad cleverly adding to his collection of dogs. We ran and shouted 'William' repeatedly to no avail. Nick blew a whistle. Nothing happened. Eventually, when we thought we had lost our friend for ever, an excitable puppy bounded back to us with the speed of a steam train at full throttle. We welcomed him with open arms as we were so relieved to be reunited with our lost pal.

After this frightening episode we decided to visit the beach.

At this time of the year many beaches were totally deserted and ideal for a wilful puppy. William adored the beach. He rushed down to the sand and dug for gold, then placed his head in the hole and did handstands, forward rolls and a selection of comical manoeuvres culminating in a mad dash for the sea before sheepishly reversing every time a wave appeared. He rolled in anything and everything from sand and seaweed to frothy foam and unpleasant detritus. He chased seagulls until he was almost out of sight, leaving us whistle-blowing and calling 'Come William' without result.

One day we visited the beautiful and mostly deserted Ker Emma beach, where in the sand dunes William made friends with Bella, a beautiful blonde female Retriever who was also one year old but two-thirds of his size. They made friends immediately and from the interest he displayed I think William would have liked to take her home. While we were walking happily towards the sea William turned and sped off towards the sand dunes where we believed he had spotted two ponies and traps. Oh dear! We could imagine him scaring the horses and overturning the traps and causing untold death and disaster. The French were unaware of their danger. We whistled and called. Nothing! He continued speeding away from us in their direction. We yelled. Eventually we saw that he was making for a collection of seagulls who immediately took flight, leaving a perplexed and bewildered dog to turn round and rush back to us for sympathy. Very relieved, we led our wild dog back to the car.

Once there he refused to clamber aboard. He had twice scrambled into the Range Rover but thereafter placed his front paws on the drop down hatch and looked around waiting for Nick to lift him in. I made sure I was very busy doing something extraordinarily important at this time, particularly if he was mucky beyond belief! Subsequently the only time he got in on his own was when Nick cunningly parked the rear of the car against a grassy bank allowing William to stroll aboard in style.

The next morning after breakfast I let William out into the walled garden while I followed him dutifully with a shovel. Suddenly he spotted yet another runner on the footpath and sprang straight over the four foot wall to freedom. Jenny from the distant 'Manoir' heard me open my lungs and yell 'William' in a voice that echoed all over Morlaix so she came to investigate. We started the hunt for William and found him on the lawn staring at an empty footpath while my heart continued to race for a fortnight.

It did not help to know that William was capable of winning the high jump when he still refused to spring into the car. We would lead him to the car saying 'Jump' in a silly sing songy encouraging tone but this was met with a refusal every time. We knew he *could* jump, which made it doubly frustrating.

When we visited Brignogan Plage we saw a guy beach-combing, accompanied by a tiny scruffy dog who himself could have benefited from a little combing. This mutt resembled a ball of black knitting that a kitten had ripped to ribbons. We led William to the other side of the beach and released the lead. All went well until he saw this ball of unkempt dread-locks run up the steps from the beach to join his master who was leaving the beach. William sped across the sand as if he had been released from a catapult and attempted to jump a ten foot wall. Then he began to leave the beach by the steps and head for the road while I ran towards him shouting 'Ah Ah!' which would have echoed all over Brittany and up into Wales. Fortunately he turned and descended the steps looking quite startled before lying down sheepishly with his paws over his ears leaving me with my poor heart pounding.

We decided that it would be best for Nick to keep William on the lead when we visited Huelgoat, where there was a freakish collection of gigantic round stones, each about the size of a Range Rover, piled on top of each other in a deep river gorge. I imagined that our wilful wonder would rush down towards the river and get stuck in the tight crevices between these huge boulders, making it well nigh impossible for us to reach him, and necessitate calling out a pet rescue party. In return for this care and concern, William became excited and strained at his lead as he wanted to explore anything and everything. When a French cyclist sped past us Wills was on fire and tried to chase the bicycle along the footpath and up a hill. It took superhuman strength to hold our powerful eleven month-old puppy, leaving Nick trembling and feeling quite shaky for the rest of the day.

The next day was cold, wet and inhospitable which meant that Nick and I were the only visitors to the delightful 'Musée de Loup' at Le Cloître St Thégonnec. This fascinating museum details, in the French language only, the story of the wolf starting with anatomy and showing how modern day dogs have descended from these wild creatures. Wolves apparently weigh between William's weight of 35Kg and 55Kg with the largest wolf weighing a massive 95Kg. Every tale and fable connected to wolves, however remotely, is recorded and we saw stunning photographs of wolves in a variety of settings, roaming the countryside, in their dens or silhouetted baying against a full moon. One delightful story concerned a man who had jumped into a pit to escape from a wolf. When the wolf joined him he spent the night playing his pipe knowing that wolves are extremely partial to a touch of tuneful melody. Apparently he was still making music when he was saved the next morning!

William could have done with a bit of melodious pipe soothing when we visited Morgat beach. A king-sized dog more wolf than Retriever came bounding over to see him. He was huge and sported the widest bull-like head I had ever seen without horns. His owner, a pretty young French girl, looked petrified and her face changed from abject terror to relief when I captured the bulky hulk for her. This canine giant was also one year old but missed an invitation to William's birthday party wholly due to size discrimination.

When we were in Landerneau Nick spotted a handbag made of wolf skin which surprisingly was being sold in a smart kitchen shop. Knowing my weakness for all things furry he secretly bought it for me and presented it to me as a 'fait accompli'. When I unwrapped my present William displayed an all-consuming interest as I think he wanted to bite it and befriend it as a prelude to breeding with it.

Ann and John, my Britanny-based friends, came over to Morlaix to visit us accompanied by their dog Alphonse who was now completely better after his road traffic accident last year. Fortunately he still loved me but rather sidelined me for his new friend, William. They gaily trotted up the railway footpath together and it was then that William invited Alphonse to his party. I never heard the response because they both rushed towards a field of black and white French cows before being neatly captured and put on leads for the rest of the walk.

Out of the two pals who were invited, William received two refusals to his first birthday party. Sadly Phoebe had to be placed in kennels whilst Stafford and Jenny returned to England for a few days, and Alphonse was busy. So to make amends we decided to buy William a birthday bone. We stopped in the car park of Le Clerc Supermarket in Lamballe and while Nick purchased the present I took William to a dog-friendly tree. I sheltered from the rain while I waited for Nick to emerge and cleverly popped the lead over a bicycle stand to prevent William from pulling. He gave up the fight and sat down and later obediently laid down. What a star! But to my horror, when he stood up his wagging tail began to paint the white wall of the supermarket jet black in a series of artistic and imaginative sweeps. He had sat in some very black gungy oil so his legs and undercarriage were covered with enough of the stuff to fill the sump of a diesel engine. Nick lifted him into the car while I hid!

We were on our way to the Museum at Laballe to see the exhibition of the renowned French artist Mathurin Meheut when we happened to pass Cathy's Pooch Parlour. This was pure serendipity. We made an immediate appointment for his 'Anniversaire' bath and missed lunch in favour of regaining a clean puppy. On the way to the Grooming Parlour, while checking his wallet for sufficient Euros, Nick unfortunately slipped off the kerb, cracking a rib and two credit cards. He was obviously shocked and suffering discomfort but he nobly battled on. We asked how long William's wash and brush up would take and when we were told 'Two and a half hours.' We asked Cathy if it was possible to take 'Une heure seulement?'. She kindly agreed. Nick was feeling fit enough to drive and visit the museum and an hour later we collected a very much paler shade of dog. His shampoo and set cost 30 Euros and was the ultimate canine birthday present. He was three times the size of the French dogs as he was bathed along with a selection of perfumed pastel poodles and petite pampered pooches of questionable pedigree. He adored all the attention and emerged not only soft, silky and sweet smelling but pedicured, backcombed and fluffed up like the biggest poofter in town, now totally hell bent on finding another mucky puddle. I, not so deftly, lifted him into the car before he could dirty any of his highly polished toenails.

On our last day in France we decided to repeat a walk in the woods near Landivisiau. Previously we had chosen a day when there was game shooting taking place so we promised ourselves a return visit this time without the fear of death or disaster. Just as we were happily close to our destination I remembered the vet. Mon Dieu! We had completely forgotten to take William to his all important appointment prior to sailing home. Without this check up we would be unable to cross the Channel. We turned round at the next motorway junction, returned to the gîte for Wills's passport and dashed to the vet just as he was closing for a two hour lunch break. He kindly gave William the necessary echinococcus injection, smeared some lotion over his neck to trouble the ticks and fool the fleas, stamped his bright blue passport and signed that he was fit to travel. Phew! We had made it just in time. William rushed out from the vet's and bounded into the car with one graceful leap, seeking refuge deep inside the boot. This was particularly galling as we had just spent three weeks lifting him in. He was so keen to leave the vet's that he could not wait for a bunk up. So he could spring in when he wanted to! We had learned another valuable lesson. From then on we would wait and wait until William was ready to jump, often leading him to the car three or four times before he cottoned on.

That afternoon Nick had a call from Brittany Ferries to say that the Roscoff to Plymouth crossing was cancelled due to bad weather so we were fortunately transferred to a larger ferry from St Malo to Portsmouth. If our ferry had been delayed, William would have had to visit the vet yet again! At St Malo we went to the Brittany Ferries Office for William to be scanned and his passport inspected. All was well so we boarded at 8pm for a sailing at 10pm. William was offered a kennel, which we refused as he was comfortable in the car on the ferry coming over. The next morning we disembarked at 8am and stopped at the first place we could find, which happened to be the Hilton Hotel, Portsmouth car park, for him to have a walk and a tired chicken and egg sandwich for breakfast!

On arriving home we dismantled the tiger cage and replaced it with the smaller travel cage from Nick's boot which made more room in my farmhouse kitchen. William refused to go in. He had sought comfort and refuge in the cage in Brittany and had often preferred to stay there rather than go on yet another long walk, but now no amount of kindly cajoling would make him enter it. I threw a treat deep into the cage. He stood there looking at it and woofed until I retrieved it! That night I decided to let him sleep on the second step of the stairs, his favourite perching place on the biggest step where it turns the corner. In the morning I found he had pee-ed on the bedding in his cage, showing in no uncertain terms what he thought of it and that he wished to be free.

From then on William became a free spirit in the kitchen whenever I had to go out to work for a few hours and also at night. He did not eat the furniture but settled down contentedly either to crash out or gnaw his bone. Provided I had shut all the doors and kept everything out of his reach, I trusted him.

William and I learned so much about puppy behaviour this year. I learned from the experience of the experts how to train a puppy and William lapped up his training as he was so eager to please. He is not perfect and never will be - but then neither am I - nor do I want to be. What we have is a special and rare relationship replete with buckets of love between 'One Gran and her Dog'. Wills is warm, affectionate and entertaining. He enhances my life and makes me smile, for he is a proper dog with an enormous zest for life and his own individual unique character. After all, he is and will always be 'William'.

AFTERTHOUGHTS

Was I barking mad to have a puppy?
After this year I have realized that a boisterous puppy, the size of a tiger, is not a suitable pet when young children come to visit occasionally. I hate to admit it but Martin, Jo and Glennis were right; not because I couldn't cope with training a puppy (I think I have done that bit to the best of my ability) or because I was away so much (fortunately Wills has been happy and well cared for at both kennels) but because my darling granddaughters were frightened by a large dog who jumped up when he was over-excited and eager to see them. Apparently dogs calm down by the time they are three years old so we have some way to go yet.

Would I have a puppy again?
If I had to choose between a cute little fluffy puppy and a well-mannered dog, I would definitely choose the adult dog, provided he was well-trained and displayed no aggressive tendencies. I would have liked to have inherited William as he is now! I could not cope with the mess in the kitchen again (now that my stone floor has recovered). The leaky stage seemed to last forever even though William was fortunate to undergo bladder and bowel training during the summer months. It was extremely disappointing when Wills was sick and unable to control his bodily functions in the car, but this stage thankfully passed with the passage of time. Life is much easier now he jumps into the car by himself and it has spared me from buying a number 69 bus!

Would I have a dog again as opposed to a bitch?
Sex makes no difference (I never thought I would say this!); obedience is vital. However, a bitch would have been less powerful and easier to handle.

AFTERTHOUGHTS

Has the expensive training made any difference?
I learned an amazing amount from Canine Etiquette, who taught me so much about training puppies or, should I say, training the owners. I learned that the important part of this schooling was consistency, similar to rearing children, so that the owner and the puppy are aware of the same rigid ground rules, such as not letting children run wild with a puppy, never leaving precious objects around, ignoring poor performance and rewarding good behaviour. By constant attention to his needs William eventually learned to empty his bladder and bowels in the garden. Waking him late at night never worked as he lay down in the garden and went to sleep! Going to the Royvon academy was great fun. It was a bonus for William to undergo expert training while I was away, which I was able to continue after each visit.

William has learned never to go upstairs (except when he was carried upstairs as a tiny puppy to show my friends on Skype!). He sits and waits impressively before all meals. He does not beg at the table nor remove objects from the working surface (though I wouldn't leave him staring at a roast chicken). He sits on command and lies down when requested nine times out of ten, but all this obedience flies out of the window when he is over-excited and away with the fairies. He comes to both his name and the whistle (unless there is a more pressing rabbit, bird or chicken to chase). He walks to a limp lead and keeps on my left hand side. He will 'fetch' a couple of time but then gets bored, although this behaviour provides us with work in progress. He has not mastered the tight rope, high jump or the forward roll; there will be no roll of drums, no musical fanfare announcing his grand entrance as he will not be appearing in any agility or beauty shows.

Is William still complete?
William has retained his testicles even though he has had a few close shaves. I learned that dogs who are incomplete still display humping skills and that it is infinitely more important to have complete control of your dog.

Would I choose a Retriever again?
Retrievers are like pussy cats without claws. All they want in

life is to be cuddled and stroked (who doesn't?). They are proper dogs. They make the most wonderfully loyal and protective companions. When I am alone in the house, I feel totally safe if William is there except perhaps at night when he barks and I have to find out who is lurking!

Would I swap William for Frankie?
No other dog, however handsome or famous, would replace the feelings and close bond I have for William. It is a privilege to be with him. He is a honey. However, I am sure that one day I will dine out on the fact that I have the brother of a Cruft's Champion.

What was my best Christmas present?
William. Thank you, Nick, with all my love.

Would I ever part with William?
Never, ever, ever.

WILLIAM'S PEDIGREE

WILLIAM	PARENTS	GRANDPARENTS
Seruilia Snowball	SIRE Gatchells Lone Ranger	SIRE **Show Champion** Marjamez Midnight Cowboy At Westervane
		DAM **SW Show Champion** Dewmist Serenella (Imp Swe)
	DAM Bedeslea Blushing Bride Via Seruilia	SIRE Seruilia Steamroller Stan
		DAM Bedeslea Black Eyed Susan

AUTHOR

Grace Dorey is a Consultant Physiotherapist at Nuffield Hospital Taunton and The Queen Street Medical Centre, Barnstaple. She also works at North Devon District NHS Hospital, Barnstaple. She is Emeritus Professor of Physiotherapy (Urology) at the University of the West of England, Bristol.

BY THE SAME AUTHOR

Clench it or Drench it! Self-help book for women with urinary leakage

Love Your Gusset: Making friends with your pelvic floor A little book for women with incontinence, sexual dysfunction and an outrageous sense of humour

Make it or Fake it! Self-help book for women with sexual dysfunction

Prevent it! Guide for men and women with leakage from the back passage

Use it or Lose it! Self-help book for men with urinary leakage and erectile dysfunction

Living and Loving After Prostate Surgery Self-help book for men with incontinence and erectile dysfunction after prostate surgery

Stronger and Longer! Guide on improving erections with pelvic floor exercises

Pelvic Dysfunction in Men: Diagnosis and Treatment of Male Incontinence and Erectile Dysfunction Textbook

Pelvic Floor Exercises for Erectile Dysfunction Textbook

All books are available from
www.yourpelvicfloor.co.uk